Be an Encourager

JAMES O. FADEL

Be an Encourager

ISBN Hardback 978-0-9895728-7-3
ISBN Paperback 978-0-9895728-5-9
eBook ISBN 978-0-9895728-6-6

Cover Design & Layout by GodKulture Publishing

Printed in the United States of America

Dedication

This book is dedicated to my wife on her 50th Jubilee Golden birthday celebration. She has graciously shared 27 of those glorious years with me.

To her I say:
You're the fairest star in my firmament:

"If you were a flower; you would be a Rose,
A Lily or a Bird of Paradise; the fairest of all flowers.
If you were a bird; you would be a Golden Pheasant, a Scarlet Macaw or a Flamingo; the fairest of all birds.
If you were a fish, you would be a Mandarin,
A Discuss or a Moorish idol, the fairest of all fishes;
Being neither a flower, a bird, nor a fish,
But created in God's own image:
You glow in His Glory and His Grace;
A specimen of God's creative ingenuity,
And the fairest star in my firmament."

On this day, June 20, 2017, I say, Happy birthday, my friend, my lover, the agave nectar in my green tea, and my wife.

I love you, so, so, so very much!

Happy birthday!

James O. Fadel

Contents

Acknowledgments

This book is tailored for all in business, secular, and spiritual organizations so we all can fulfill our purpose on earth.

I acknowledge the editorial input of Pst. Laolu Akande, Pst. William Ekanem, Pst. Sayo Ajiboye, and Pst. Daps Zion. A team of amiable people like Olajumoke Lawal, Funmi Adeyemi, members my staff in the office and others; you are all a source of encouragement to me and by His Grace, you will all impact your generation for Jesus.

I appreciate my wife, my three beautiful, talented, and smart biological children and thousands of spiritual children who have encouraged and motivated me to finish my work. Thank you for being in the community of encouragers.

I love you all.

Law of Magnetism

The law of magnetism states that "who we are is who we attract." The recently concluded 2017 Superbowl between Atlanta Falcons and New England Patriots perfectly illustrates this law. When the Falcons were ahead, you could see the fans screaming and becoming nearly delirious because of their lead. However, it seems as if they were waiting for the other shoe to fall off. The Patriots fans on the other hand kept having faith, they kept on cheering and kept on believing their team will win.

It was obvious that the Patriots have a higher expectation. They were not better than the Falcons because they have won four Superbowl in the past and this would be their fifth. The higher expectation was due to the law of magnetism. They have seen and experienced their team win before, and they believed that they are in a winning environment. Living in a positive atmosphere creates an expectancy that that leads to a win, while immersing oneself in a losing environment almost guarantees a life filled with failures.

Many leaders who could be winners in business, church or mission fail for lack of encouragement and the absence of being cheered on by someone who believes in them. Equally, many only keep going and ultimately win because someone does come alongside to cheer them on and shouts when they make it.

You can win, and you will win! It takes one match to start a fire, and it takes one person to believe, cheer and encourage you to win. You can win, and please go and win!

HAVE YOU EVER NEEDED ENCOURAGEMENT?

We all know what it means to be down, disappointed,

stabbed in the back, or accused falsely. We all know what it's like for someone to come alongside you who understands, pulls you up, and says, I'll walk with you, pray with you, and I understand what you're going through. Aaaah …what a relief!

To be an encourager is to fulfill God's mandate and ensure we play our part so that others can fulfill their purpose. We speak to all in business, community, churches, and the world at large that you're here on earth to help encourage others to fulfill their God given mandate on earth.

May I ask you, how are you doing?

The good news is that God is in the business of encouraging people, giving people a second, third, fourth, and as many chances it requires for them to come back. He gives hope to the hopeless, direction to the direction-less. He is called the God of all encouragement. God's plan for you is to give you hope and a future!

- Deuteronomy 3:28," But charge Joshua, and encourage him, and strengthen him: for he shall go over before this people, and he shall cause them to inherit the land which thou shalt see."

- Mark 3:17," And James the son of Zebedee, and John the brother of James; and he surnamed them Boanerges, which is, The sons of thunder"

- Are you Boanerges, "sons of thunder" or Barnabas , son of Consolation (encouragement)?

- Acts 4:36," And Joses, who by the apostles was surnamed Barnabas, (which is, being interpreted, The son of consolation,) a Levite, and of the country of Cyprus."

Foreword

by Elder Felix O. A. Ohiwerei

When I received the manuscript of the book *Be an Encourager* from Pastor James Fadel, I opened it with haste to get a first impression. I just wanted to get a feel of the book. That was not to be. By the time I closed my iPad, I had spent well over one hour. I could not tear myself away easily.

In this book, Pastor James Fadel has given a meaning and dimension to the word "Encourage" which will give every kingdom-minded person a good reason to reflect on his/her use of words. It portrays clearly the potential in each of us to build or destroy with our words (Proverbs 18:21).

The title, **Be an Encourager**, reminded me of what happened when God appointed Joshua to lead the nation of Israel after the death of Moses (Joshua 11:1-8). Joshua, the servant to Moses, suddenly found himself with a daunting responsibility.

a. The first thing God did was to encourage Joshua: "There shall not any man be able to stand before thee all the days of thy life. As I was with Moses, so I will be with thee: I will not fail thee nor forsake thee" (Verse 5).

b. The second thing was to give Joshua the formula for good success:

i. "Be strong and of a good courage…" (Verse 6)

ii. "Only be thou strong and very courageous that thou mayest observe to do according to all the law, which Moses My servant commanded you …" (Verse 7).

iii. "This book of the law shall not depart out of thy mouth; but thou shall meditate therein day and night…" (Verse 8).

The sequence of events here demonstrates the importance of courage and encouragement. God knew that Joshua had been taught by Moses to trust Him and His word. But God also knew that Joshua needed to be encouraged.

In a well-researched, scholarly, and realistic manner, this book convincingly deals with such issues as who needs to be encouraged, the sources of encouragement, the God of all Encouragement, the power of Encouraging words, Sources of Encouragement, Dangers of Discouragement, etc.

Do you know that there is a cultural dimension to Encouragement? This book has a lot to offer the enquiring mind on this subject. I found it fascinating.

There are many important lessons from this excellent book. One of them is the role encouraging words and actions play in assisting Christians to end well. In an age when the concentration is on self, it is important to be reminded that the legacy that lasts is that which builds people and not that which builds mansions. The encourager is a builder of good and lasting relationships. This book reminds us that life is about relationships – with our Creator, parents, siblings, schoolmates, etc.

To all those who are kingdom minded, *Be an Encourager* is a must read.

I have been mightily blessed by it. I am sure it will be a blessing to you too.

Elder Felix O. A. Ohiwerei

First Words

by Olayinka Dada M.D., FCFP, PhD

Senior Pastor, RCCG Restoration House, Hamilton, Canada

Regional Pastor, RCCG NAR- 10

It is a great honor for me to write the foreword to the book "Be an Encourager." Times and today's values are constantly changing. There is insecurity and enormous fear everywhere. These have resulted in the levels of disease and destructive behavior we see now.

There are too many dysfunctional families, suicide rates are on the increase, divorce is rampant, life expectancy is going down, drug abuse is also escalating, too many juvenile delinquents are rising up, and the list goes on and on. Many of these can be prevented if someone can be an encourager to a troubled or lonely soul.

Everyone needs encouragement. Life will be exciting when there are continual words of encouragement flying around you. I have been discouraged several times in my life. I have been wounded by friends or close associates and I have been able to come out stronger because of the support structure in my life. I thank God for my wife, who has always been a great source of encouragement to me and brings out the best in me.

I have been blessed to have had contacts with and learn from many other wonderful encouragers, and I have realized that you can maximize your potential and run the human race with excellence when you have encouragers in your life.

Pastor James Fadel is one of the great encouragers I have met. He is soft spoken and quick to encourage people around him. To have an encourager write about the impact of encouragement is indeed encouraging.

I strongly believe that this book is birthed out of the experiences of leading over seven hundred pastors in our phenomenal church: The Redeemed Christian Church of God, North America.

I can certainly say about this powerful book, Be Encouraged that:

It will bless your life
It will revive your soul and spirit
It will transform your mind
It will open you up for a new level of greatness
It will make you an encourager too

This book is an easy read and it invites everyone to come up higher by understanding the impact of encouragement in fulfilling destiny and making you a blessing to others. Encouragement works just as prayer works. It is satisfying and refreshing to every soul.

Happy reading!

Olayinka Dada M.D., FCFP, PhD
Senior Pastor, RCCG Restoration House, Hamilton, Canada
Regional Pastor, RCCG NAR- 10

Introduction

Daily, life throws challenges, disappointments, and heartaches our way. These difficulties and frustrations can make us disillusioned and even depressed. It is for this reason that everyone at one point in time or the other needs some form of encouragement to be inspired and to lift their spirit.

Encouragement is a concept as old as mankind. It is always in high demand by the individual, families, groups, communities, and even nations who are committed to growth and experiencing progress.

Life without encouragement is unimaginable. Such a life would be meaningless, burdensome, and discouraging. There would be no willpower to forge ahead; people would be continuously overwhelmed, and they would feel unloved. Encouragement gives us strength; it helps us to focus on the bigger picture; encouragement builds patience and hopes inside our hearts. Every human appreciates some form of encouragement. It can come from the scriptures, or it can come from the simple empathy of wise neighbors.

The title of this book is **Be An Encourager**. We will dig deeper into the concept of encouragement. We will draw substantial wisdom from the word of God. We will consider the lives of individuals who were encouraged, and we will bring out lessons from these two sources.

The first chapter delves into the concept of encouragement. Who are the givers and the receivers and how does it affect an individual's response to the vicissitudes of life? This chapter treats encouragement as the central theme of the Bible. In this Chapter, we use the Ninth hour statement of Jesus during his tribulations, for the offense that he did not commit, to understanding the power of "Encouragement." Even the Savior needed encouragement in his time of trial. In

Mark 15:34, Jesus uttered this agonizing cry: "Eloi Eloi, lama sabachthani." This is translated: "My God, My God, why have you forsaken me?" Encouragement from the scriptures inspires people to cope with everyday challenges. The ninth hour cry shows that everybody needs encouragement regardless of their position or their status.

Encouragement must address the body, soul, and spirit of the individual. Hebrews 3:13, enjoins us to "encourage one another daily, while it is still called today, lest any of you be hardened through the deceitfulness of sin." This chapter will show how we can fulfill these words.

The next chapter deals with God's character as the source of all encouragement. Readers may ask the question, "How can God be the One who permits stress and trouble to come and at the same time provide the beacon of hope for those in need of help?" This chapter answers the question by exploring God's intervention in the affairs of man from the Old to the New Testament. In this Chapter, we show that amid the travails of life, one needs encouragement to cope.

The second chapter contrasts God's perspective on encouragement with man's perspective. The chapter points out examples where man attempted to encourage himself as David did. We also look at attempts by friends and family to encourage an individual, like in the case of Jacob in Genesis 37:35. Human encouragement can never be sufficient except when the Holy Spirit takes over the task. It is for this very reason that the Holy Spirit is known as the Comforter (John 14:26).

Chapter Three focuses on the power of encouraging words. Words have an impact and encouraging words can make the difference between life and death, success and failure. We reason with King Solomon who said: "a soft answer turns away wrath. But a harsh word stirs up anger," (Proverbs 15:1).

Imagine the absence of the popular five "magic" words of please, thank you, sorry, excuse me and pardon me.

Psychologists say that these words help to reduce 78% of potential troubles. We will examine the power of these words and their ability to assist humans in avoiding senseless fights over time. This position draws credence from the scriptures that "the mouth of the righteous is a well of life" and that "violence covers the mouth of the wicked" (Proverbs 10:11).

Chapter Four focuses on sources of encouragement, and it revolves around 1 Thessalonians 5:11. This passage gives all humans the assignment to "Therefore encourage one another and build each other up, just as in fact you are doing." We will look at the roles of spouses, parents, children, prophets, preacher's friends (what does "preacher's friends" mean?), family, and associates as sources of encouragement.

We will also look at Divine encouragement. God's promise to mankind in Isaiah 51:3 is the basis for an expectation of Divine encouragement. We will examine the various forms of encouragement listed in Leo Buscaylia's saying: "Too often we underestimate the power of a touch, a smile, a kind word, a listening ear, an honest compliment or the smallest act of caring, all of which have the potential to turn a life around."

When the forms of encouragement in the list above are not forthcoming, discouragement sets in and the individual begins to give in or give up. Depression and, perhaps, backsliding begin.

Chapter Five is on the dangers of discouragement. It gives examples of people in and outside the Bible who were bitten by the bug of discouragement.

When Nehemiah mobilized the residents of Jerusalem to build a wall around the entire city of Jerusalem, the project looked harmless, innocent, and rather simple. Nehemiah would have thought that within a few weeks, he would complete the project and go back to Persia to resume his governorship. However, half way through the project, the citizens became discouraged and wanted to give up. The great prophet Moses also experienced discouragement when no one encouraged him in the face of God's decree that he will not enter the Promised Land. The Prophet Elijah asked to die in the face of deep discouragement, and at Gethsemane, Jesus our Lord felt deeply discouraged. Demas abandoned Paul, and many other situations in the Scriptures show great servants of God facing discouragement. The chapter looks at such moments of discouragement and discusses how they were all overcome.

Encouragement lifts the challenged and inspires the hopeless. Those who receive encouragement always end well. Jesus ended well partly because angels ministered to him. David and Paul encouraged themselves in the Lord, and they ended well. The saints at Philippi encouraged Paul, and he ended well. Certain individuals in our times almost lost out, but someone encouraged them, and they finished well.

We will ask ourselves if encouragement can be culture specific. We will examine the unique roles that exist for different demographic groups in various cultures. We will question whether encouragement is learned, acquired, or transferred.

The Apostle Paul summed up these cultural questions in Ephesians 4:29: "do not let unwholesome [foul, profane, worthless, vulgar] words ever come out of your mouth, but only such speech as is good for building up others, according to the need and the occasion, so that it will be a blessing to those who hear [you speak]," (AMP).

We will ask ourselves how believers in Christ respond to this great counsel within the culture.

We will consider the cultural dimension in Chapter Seven. We will seek to know to what extent scriptures, counsel, and indeed tradition influence encouragement.

The apostles of Jesus Christ and all other martyrs operated outside their comfort zones. Trials and tribulations characterized their various ministries. However, rather than discourage them, their circumstances propelled them to service, doing undeniably notable deeds (Acts 4:16).

We will learn how to turn our mess into a message. We will find out how to turn our tests to testimonies. The power of encouragement will lift us from the grounds of dismay to the mountain tops of our endeavors. The power of encouragement in the concluding pages of this book will propel us into a secure future that is fearless. God's mighty grace will gloriously wrap around our lives.

Chapter Eight addresses the issue of the life of service as an encouragement to others. Service, especially sacrificial service, is very encouraging. We will explore this in the story of Rebecca. She not only gave Eliezer, Abraham's servant, water to drink, but she also fetched gallons of water for the camels, and in so doing, she ended up as Isaac's wife. We will consider this instructive story and that of other men of God. We will consider the stories of the Apostles, who did not serve in comfort zones, but their calling paid off for them.
Each chapter will end with Prayer Points, Lessons Learned, and Action Points to assist the reader in his or her meditation on the contents of the book.

CHAPTER ONE

Everyone Needs Encouragement

"Eloi Eloi, lama sabachthani," which is translated, "My God, My God, why have you forsaken me?" (Mark 15:34), is a statement of anguish and despondency. In the dying moments of Jesus Christ, in the ninth hour of his tribulations, amid suffering for offenses he did not commit, the agony of his soul made him cry out.

As he was battered and abused by the Roman soldiers, Jesus called on his father for encouragement. What followed was even worse as one of the soldiers filled a sponge with vinegar, according to the scriptures, and made him drink.

If there was anything that Jesus needed at that moment, it was encouragement, but no man could have encouraged

Jesus at this time because the arm of the flesh must fail for God to be glorified. Jesus cried unto his father in heaven. When you are choked by the worries of life, to whom do you cry?

Jesus did not cry to people around him; the people around him, including his disciples, could not do much to help him. Jesus cried to his father in the face of those who doubled down on the affront and abuse. The people ridiculed him and claimed that he was calling on Elias to come bail him out.

The other day, I asked a church sister why she was not in church; she responded that she woke up with severe body pains. The husband had left for work with their only car, and she had three little children and her aged mother to prepare for church. Before she finished with that, it was just too late to make it to church that Sunday.

Are there days like that when you can relate to our sister's circumstances? Are there days when you have a splitting headache, body pains, and yet you have so many responsibilities that you must address? It is possible that you may be feeling that way even as you read this book.

Some days are just very challenging. From the moment you regain consciousness in the morning, events and activities just show that it's going to be an interesting day. You suddenly have so many issues to cope with. Life pummels us with disappointments, ridicule, humiliations, and even abandonment. These experiences affect our emotions and make us very discouraged.

When you are at this juncture, how do you push through? Do you feel bad and get disillusioned, or do you keep moving and shake it off ?

At such moments, everyone needs some form of encouragement and inspiration to get going. We require assistance in pulling ourselves out of the pit of negativity. We need to replace negative thoughts and conclusions with faith inspiring ideas and feelings.

The danger here is to leave the negative dealings and not address them. Such negligence will affect the physical well-being of the individual. This physical well-being is a reason why it is necessary to ask often after each other. We must ask the question "Are you okay?" We must be empathetic and sometimes say "You don't look well." When emotions and feelings weigh on the looks of an individual, it's a sign of being overwhelmed by life's situations. It becomes self-evident that such an individual needs encouragement.

But what is "encouragement" and who needs it?

Matt Perman defines encouragement as the giving of courage, hope, confidence, support, and help. It is the act of giving an individual or people the courage, spirit, and hope to inspire.

Others see encouragement as comfort, confidence, or persuasion to do something. Scripturally, the Apostle Paul, according to Perman, ties the act of encouragement to the process of building up one another, as contained in 1 Thessalonians 5:11, "Therefore encourage one another and build each other up, just as in fact you are doing."

Perman's point of view is that we can aid our understanding of the word to encourage by looking at the gift of encouragement (or exhortation) as stated in Romans 12:8. Students of the Greek language indicate the word comes from the same family of words used to describe the Holy Spirit as our Paraclete, "one who comes alongside us to help." Leslie B. Flynn wrote of encouragement as helping to strengthen the weak, to steady the faltering, and to console the troubled.

Scriptural encouragement is often closely aligned with restoration and renewal of Spirit. For example, in Psalm 3, David reflected on the horrible experience of having his son turn against him. It caused such a rift that all of

David's relationships were broken. The Psalm indicates, among other things, that God replenished David's courage (encouragement), restored his confidence (depleted by his experience), and revived his hope. Some of the same results will accrue from our involvement in encouraging others.

Theological review of 42 New Testament references reveals that within the word encourage is a ministry for all believers. Some individuals may have special abilities because of God's gifting, but all individuals need encouragement. All individuals need someone who will come alongside him or her to offer help and hope.

Encouragement can impact many people as one individual either shares his or her experience or talks about it. Truett Cathy, the founder of Chick-Fil-A, has always maintained that he wasn't in the chicken business, but in a people business. From knowing his customers by name to forming lifelong friendships with his employees, Cathy viewed his business as more than a source of revenue for him and his family; it was a source of encouragement to others.

In the same vein, Anthony Cardinal Okogie, Ecclesiastical Archbishop emeritus of Lagos, wrote a passionate letter to the President of Nigeria, his country, on a national issue. He appealed to the president to urge his lieutenants to show forms of encouragement to the citizenry in the face of harsh economic realities.

In the letter, the Catholic priest said, "The introduction of town hall meetings is a commendable idea. But in practice, you, not just your ministers, must converse with Nigerians. You are the President. You must be accountable to them. The buck stops on your desk. Even if your administration has no magic wand, at least give some words of encouragement. On this same score, please instruct your ministers, and insist that they be sincere and polite at those town meetings. Their sophistry will neither serve you nor Nigerians,"

Here, the cardinal harped on the need for ministers to give

the people some form of encouragement, although things may not have been as good as the people wanted. I see encouragement as a form of praise, support, boost, lift, and endorsement that we give either to an individual, group, or organization. It is a process to ensure success.

In Luke 7, Jesus encouraged the widow whose son had just died and was on the way to be buried. Jesus showed up and encouraged the woman with the words, "don't cry." Jesus even went further and raised the widow's son from death.

There couldn't have been a better encouragement for the widow who was distraught over the death of her only son. This was probably her companion and the house-mate that she depended on in her old age. The death of this only son could only be the most discouraging thing. On the way to the burial of the dead son, however, Jesus Christ showed up. He is the God of time and chance, and he showed up.

Are you discouraged as you read this book? Do you think that all is lost? It is not too late. God can show up and turn the tide of whatever you are going through.

In the widow's circumstances, Jesus showed up with two things: empathy and power.

With empathy, Jesus encouraged the woman by telling her not to cry, not to weep. It is in the same manner that the King of Kings is telling you now, "weep not, dry your tears for I am not as far as you think." Acts 17:27 says God is not as far as we think.

Jesus showed up with power. Ephesians 6:10 talks of the power of his might. Jesus touched the bier, and the bearers stopped. Exodus 6:6 tells us of the power of His outstretched arm.

Today the Lord, with His right hand, will touch your situation, and the bleeding will stop. The shame will stop. The attack will stop.

The opposition, the drift into nothingness, will stop, in the name of Jesus.

When Jesus spoke, the power went with His word; the scriptures say in Mathew 7:29 and Luke 4:32 that "He speaks with authority." As you read this now, take time out and have this word of prayer: Lord, please speak to my circumstances, my job, career, finance, immigration, barrenness today.

The good news is this: When Jesus shows up to encourage anyone, He turns around every negative circumstance that makes the individual cry. He turns disappointment to an appointment with destiny. He changes the messy situation into a message to those who trust in Him. He turns the test to testimony. As you read this book and you believe, all that Jesus does will be your portion.

Who needs encouragement?

Practically every living soul needs encouragement. Even Jesus, while on earth in a human form, needed encouragement in Mark 15:34 when he was persecuted. Life is not a bed of roses. Job 14:1 shows us that trouble, or in using a refined word, challenges, would always be there for the individual, family, or nation. So everyone will need some form of encouragement at some time or the other.

The co-founder of Chick-Fil-A, Dan Cathy, is known for his famous words, which still ring in the conversations of those who knew him: "How do you know someone needs encouragement? If they're breathing!" This is a clear indication that every living individual needs encouragement.

Nancy Leigh DeMoss, in a series tagged, *Revive Our Hearts*, points out that we're supposed to be helping each other and encouraging each other so that those seeds of discouragement don't put down roots and turn into full-blown depression and anger and violence as it happens in so many lives, even in the church today.

I want us together to come up with a list here. Please add your own to it. Write down several categories of people who need to be encouraged. Jot these down and jot down anyone that comes to your mind. Do think of someone who is in any of these categories that need to be encouraged.

Family Members

Struggling Students

Working Young Adults

Young Mothers

Families with Financial Issues

Families with Sick Members

....

....

....

....

As we think about this issue, God will put on your heart one or two or maybe three people who need someone to encourage them. They need some helping hands. They need someone to come alongside them and live out what it means to encourage or to exhort.

We're to encourage one another daily. Ask the Lord to impress on your heart the person He has put in your life that He (the Lord) wants you to make an intentional effort to encourage.

We must start with our families. It's hypocritical for us to be trying to encourage everyone else in the world and then be discouragers inside the four walls of our homes. So, let me ask you to think about this issue: "Do you encourage people outside your home more than you do the people who live in your home?"

Now, I think all of us, if we're honest, would have to say sometimes it's easier to encourage people outside our homes than it is to encourage the people we live with all the time because that's where we let our hair down. That's where we don't worry as much about manners, though we should. That is where we often do not think about how we affect each other, though we should. Sometimes we're just tired of the people we live with. The people we go to church with or the people that we work with, well, we can muster up what it takes to encourage them.

The starting place for the ministry of encouragement should be in our homes. And let me suggest you start with your parents. Realize that God wants us to honor our parents. We must all do this act regardless of age, regardless of whether your parents are believers or not, regardless of whether they have a heart for God or not, regardless of whether your parents were good parents or bad parents, we are to honor our parents. Encouragement is a very important way that we honor our parents.

If it is right, then you must find the time to do it. It may be that you haven't connected with your parents for a long period, and you've been waiting for them to come back and give you the encouragement that they never gave as you were growing up. Don't wait for them to come to you. You humble yourself. Go to them and ask God for ways you can encourage your parents. Put something back into their lives as they have put many things into your life over the years.

After starting with your parents, there may be siblings that you need to encourage, even adult siblings. After this sibling issue, then there is your mate. Wives, can I just say that your husband needs you to be his number one cheerleader? And can I also say, if you are not going to be an encourager in his life, there are plenty of other women who will? You must be the number one encourager in your husband's life.

Even though the lack of encouragement is no justification, it is no wonder that so many marriages are breaking up today.

When a man goes into his workplace, he can find women who will fall all over themselves to encourage him. They will listen. They will care. They will show concern. They will show appreciation and admiration, and then he comes home to a discouraging, whining, dripping faucet for a wife!

Now, maybe she's doing that out of her discouragement, but I want to offer this counsel: if you want to keep your marriage intact, you must ask God to help you to know how to encourage your husband. Your home should be a place where your husband can come and be safe. It must be a place where he can have a refuge, a place where he can have someone to build him up and strengthen him.

If you are married, your husband should be the number one person to look for ways to encourage. And may I just put a parenthesis here: you ought to be encouraging your husband and being cautious and careful about how you encourage somebody else's husband. You may be in the workplace with a man you look up to and you respect. You're only seeing him at work. You don't live with him. You may think you'd like to, but you don't live with him.

There are appropriate ways for women to encourage other women's husbands, and there are also ways that step over the line. God will give you wisdom as to how never to cross the line. Allow me to share one of the things that has worked for me as a safeguard. If I want to encourage a man of God, a pastor or somebody that I'm working with who has blessed my life, I try to get the couple together, and I let them both know what a blessing or encouragement they are to me or how much I appreciate them. I will state what I appreciate about their lives and their ministry. This process provides an appropriate way to communicate encouragement to someone else's husband. Get the wife involved and encourage her as well.

Your encouragement can make such a difference in your husband's life and in the way that he encourages you in turn.

Now, you don't want to encourage him in a manipulative way so that you can get what you want. I think of a lady who wrote to one of our partner ministries of *Revive Our Hearts.* She shared that she had approached her husband several times about attending a marriage conference together. This Conference is something she wanted to do, and he clearly communicated that he was not interested. So, she, wisely, dropped the topic.

But then she told in her letter of how a year ago she started a journal to encourage her husband with all the things that he does as a father for their two children. She presented this to him as a Father's Day present, just a journal of things she had written down that she had noticed about how he was such a great father to their kids. She wasn't even thinking about the marriage conference at that point. She was just trying to be an encourager.

And she wrote to say that, "I didn't expect that it would touch him as much as it did. Little by little my husband began to be more expressive about how he feels about me and how much I mean to him. These are the little things I've always longed for and treasured most in our relationship."

Then she tells the story of how he came to her at one point after getting this journal. Christmas was approaching, and he said, "What do you want for Christmas?"

She just said, "I've got everything that I need." She couldn't think of anything.

He pressed her, and he finally said to her, "What about that marriage conference you've wanted to go to? Could we sign up for that?" He said this would be her Christmas and their twentieth wedding anniversary present.

She was writing to one of our partner ministries to say how thankful she was that God had given her the idea to be an encourager to her husband. She showed how a simple, little idea of that encouragement journal filled with appreciation and attention and admiration, ministered to her husband in such a way that he turned around and wanted to be an encouragement to his wife.

Doug Britton corroborated this position with this personal testimony, "I always am encouraged when my wife praises me. This truth came home to me once in a graphic, although silly, way. We used to take our sons to a video arcade, and I often played my favorite game. It soon became obvious that my scores were much higher whenever my wife watched and cheered me on."

"Encourage one another daily," Hebrews 3 says, "so that none of your hearts will become hardened by the deceitfulness of sin."

Think up some other categories of people we need to encourage. Start with your family and say, "Lord, is there someone in my home, one of my children, my mate, my parents, my in-laws, extended family members, who I need to encourage? Who have You put in my path that needs encouragement right now?" Then ask God to show you how to do that.

Encouragement is not a time or place specific, and it should be all encompassing. It should span every aspect of our physical beings, and even soul and spirit.

Now, let's borrow Dan Cathy's account to see how encouragement can span through body, soul, and spirit:

"I went through the drive through once on an awful day when everything was wrong. My sister in law was in hospice and dying, my youngest had been diagnosed with dyslexia, and my oldest was flunking out of college. It was obvious I had been crying when I got to the window to get my order. She passed me my food and instead of saying have a nice day (these people are always so sweet), she reached through the window and patted my arm and said: "I don't know what is going, but I know it WILL get better, hang in there." At that moment, it was like a voice from God and the most calming, encouraging words and itgave me the strength to pull myself together, and I will never forget how it did help me."

This is a personal account of someone amid daunting experiences and facing despondency. This is an individual who is trying to power through the vicissitudes of life. He got real encouragement from this one quarter that you least expect it.

Some people when afflicted do not even have the appetite to eat. Dan Cathy was still able to go for food to keep the body together. Elijah, on the other hand, needed angelic encouragement to eat "for the journey is far", 1 Kings 19:7. Cathy encouraged himself by not forgoing food. The human body functions better when encouraged; otherwise, we would not have supporters cheering on during sporting competitions for instance.

The fast food attendant spoke the needed words at that point in time to Cathy. "I don't know what is going, but I know it WILL get better, hang in there." These may not be scriptures from the Bible, but they sure meet the instruction from the Apostle Paul that we should "encourage one another and build each other up, just as in fact you are doing" (1 Thessalonians 5:11). The Scriptures are replete with spiritual instructions of this nature. They enjoin us to encourage each other daily. When such encouraging words come, they go straight to the inner being, and they touch the soul of the receiver.

Cathy's reaction to the encouragement by the food attendant corroborates this fact. According to him, it was like a voice from God. It went through his system to calm him, and it gave him the needed lifting as at that point in time. That was why the Apostle Paul encouraged the people in Corinth in his second letter 4:17, "for our light and momentary troubles are achieving for us an eternal glory that far outweighs them all." This type of comfort goes beyond the body and touches the spirit, and it goes deep down to revive the soul of a practicing Christian.

CHAPTER TWO

The God of all Encouragement

No one encourages better than God; that is why the scriptures call God the "Father of compassion and the God of all comfort who comfort those in ANY trouble" (2 Corinthians 1:3-4). The entire plan of God to reconcile man unto Himself hinges on the awesome nature of God to encourage man to keep the faith.

Man lost it initially. He lost it through a combination of emotive forces such as anger, hatred, and animosity towards fellow men. God, however, encouraged man through his only son. He reconciled us towards him so that we are not hardened by the deceitfulness of sin.

Nancy Deboss, in her series *Encouraging One Another*, points out that the book of Hebrews was written to encourage the new Jewish believers in their faith and in their walk with God. Nancy puts it this way: "The book of Hebrews is written to Hebrew believers, believers in Christ who were suffering for their faith, who were experiencing the challenges of being a very small minority in a hostile environment, and they needed courage. They needed encouragement."

They were living in a world that was not sympathetic to their faith. The Jews didn't accept Christ as the Messiah. The Gentiles, on the other hand, rejected a Jewish faith. And here was this small band of Jewish believers, and they were trying to walk with God. They needed to know the gospel and the ways of God. They needed to be aware of the heart of God to encourage them in their faith. God was committed to encouraging these believers to be faithful and to persevere when everything around them was discouraging them from going on in their faith.

Therefore, encouragement originated from creation with God encouraging mankind in the face of daunting experiences. It is in the light of this that Jesus told his disciples, shortly before been crucified, "In this world, you will have trouble; but take heart, I have overcome the world." John 16: 33

God's perspective of encouragement is not a promise of an unending honeymoon for believers on earth. God is not interested in having individuals frolic in their comfort zones without any duty and or sense of responsibility. God made it very clear that anyone that follows Him must not only count the cost, but also carry his or her cross daily. Although Jesus meant more than the problems we encounter in our daily lives in this statement, it must also be acknowledged that in Jesus' days, the cross was a symbol of suffering. Today, we all have trials and afflictions that we pass through in the journey of life.

Little wonder Job said, "man who is born of a woman is of few days and full of trouble," Job 14:1. Job exposed the calamitous state of human life: it is short-lived, filled with sadness, very few days, and full of trouble. For many people, they are not only troubled, but their life is full of toiling or fretting, grieving or fearing. This challenging state is the reason why so many verses of the Bible are focused on God's promises that encourage the believer.

Jesus did not mince words in telling His followers about troubles they would face. He went as far as giving them a hint that the world would hate them (John 15:18-21). Although, it is true that his grim forecast is often tempered with loving words of encouragement of faith, hope, and words of love that balance the present grievance.

God's perspective of encouragement reminds us always of one truth: God loves us. God equips us daily to function efficiently. God treasures us; our struggles and our faith in Him are worth it. God wishes above all things that we may prosper and be in good health, even as our soul prospers. It is with this perspective that we now consider God's way of encouraging us to have hope, practice love, and remain holy.

God's Encouragement Builds Hope: God encourages us with hope for now and hereafter. Regardless of what happens, the Scripture encourages believers not to grieve like those who have no hope (1 Thessalonians 4:13). This is because when hope is lost, enthusiasm is gone, and negativity sets in. As John Mason stated, "the negative person is half-defeated before even beginning."

God's words comfort us in whatever we are passing through. The Apostle Paul puts it this way, "for whatever things were written for our learning, that we through the patience and comfort of the scriptures might have hope" (Romans 15:4). The phrase "comfort of the scripture," in the above verse is a ministration on its own, it is the theme of this chapter, and the idea runs through the entire book.

The comfort of the Scriptures calls us to put our hope in the word of God, to believe it, and to run with it. Take for instance a passage like John 10:10, Isaiah 43:2, or Isaiah 49:13. There are also many others passages that encourage us during afflictions.

Consider also, the use of the words patience and comfort in Paul's letter referenced above. They presuppose that there may be times when all is not well in our faith journey. There would be trouble, sorrow, headache, and inconveniences as a lot of believers. The only sure panacea is the comforting words from God that give hope.

Think about this: what does the word hope mean to you? The meaning could vary as much as those defining it. However, biblical hope is usually based on our faith and the assurances in God's words; it has a foundation in God. The biblical hope triumphs in the face of uncertainty, trouble, and not just in the comfort zones. It is characterized by joy, it has zero melancholic content. The Apostle Paul referred to this joy in Romans 5:1: "having been justified by faith, we have peace with God through our Lord Jesus Christ; through whom also we have access by faith into his grace in which we stand and rejoice in the hope of the glory of God."

The hope in Christ is a joyful one. It does not depend on the circumstance. James summed it up as follows: "count it all joy when you fall into various trials" (James 1:1). The psalmist encourages us to sing songs of praises. Paul and Silas practiced this during their tribulation in Phillipi.

When we achieve this level of consciousness of the word, then we can "glory in tribulations, knowing that tribulation produces perseverance, and perseverance, character and character, hope" (Romans 5:3). My prayer is that God will take us to that level in Jesus name.

God's Encouragement Enhances Love: I once heard a barber shop discussion. It always comes to mind each time love is discussed. Even though I was a silent listener in the discussion, I have never stopped thinking about it. The barber in this discussion said that love is not learned but that it comes naturally, while hate is learned and nurtured.

According to the barber, we were born to love. He used the example of little children that innocently love everybody and everything until they grow up. After growing up, they develop self-consciousness and begin to draw lines in relating with people. As I thought about it, I remember how growingup as a kid, my parents, who were seeking to genuinely protect me, would caution me on who to play with. I vividly remember that I was told not to have anything to do with one of our neighbor's, who was also a family member, because the father was an alcoholic and his young children were always caught smoking cigarettes.

Although my parents meant well, and they were guiding against my keeping bad company, they inadvertently taught me to avoid our neighbor's children; in other words, I was to have nothing to do with them.

The Bible is replete with God's words on love. 1 Corinthians 14:1 instructs us, "let love be your greatest aim," We are born for love, and we are born to love. Love opens doors and removes limitations. Everything should be done with love. We must ask this question: where exactly should we exhibit our love? God encourages us to extend our love to Himself, to our neighbors, and even to our enemies.

We must always remember that love begins with God because God is love. He loves His son Jesus Christ, who was sinless, and He also loves the world despite its sinfulness. The reason He sent His only Son as an atoning sacrifice was to show the depth of His love.

We are made in God's image, and God encourages us to emulate Him in love. We emulate Him through selflessness and self- sacrifice. God has set the race of life before all of us, to make the race less tedious, God collapsed all commandments intojust one: love! "For the commandments, you shall not commit adultery, you shall not murder, you shall not steal, you shall not bear false witness, you shall not covet, and if there is any other commandment, are all summed up in this saying, namely, you shall love your neighbor as yourself." Romans 13:9

We must take love very seriously because it is the first and highest of all Christian virtues. It is even greater than faith and hope. (I Corinthians 13:13). Mathew Henry's Commentary explains that while faith fixes itself on the divine revelation and assents to that, hope fastens itself on future blessedness, and waits for that, but love fastens on the divine perfections themselves.

The scriptures encourage us "not to love in word or in tongue, but indeed and in truth" (1 John 3:18). We are encouraged to love one another, for love is of God, and everyone who loves is born of God and knows God (I John 4:7).

By loving one another, we are loving God. The Scripture says: "no one has seen God at any time. If we love one another, God abides in us, and His love has been perfected in us" (1 John 4:12).

The word of God makes us understand that nothing shall separate us from the love of Christ, if we abide in Him. All the discouraging factors of this world, tribulation, distress, persecution, famine, or danger, cannot separate us. His love will make us more than conquerors (Romans 8:35-38).

Here then lies the secret to overcoming every discouraging situation: The love of God and the love of the man who God created. I strongly recommend that you should fully subscribe to love for, "by this, all will know that you are my disciples, if you have love for one another" (John 13:35).

God's Encouragement Enhances Holiness

A recurring theme of the Bible is a call to holiness. God used his words to encourage us to be holy. What is holiness? Holiness is to be set apart for God. Leviticus 11:45 says, "For I am the Lord who brings you up out of the land of Egypt, to be your God. You shall, therefore, be holy, for I am holy."

God's children are encouraged to keep growing in holiness. This growth occurs as we separate ourselves from sin in our everyday life. "Pursue peace with all people, and holiness, without which no one will see the Lord" (Hebrews 12:14). Holiness is for our own good and holiness brings glory to God.

The benefits of holiness are immeasurable. Kathy Howard, who runs a Christian ministry that helps women live an unshakeable faith for life, no matter the circumstance, listed benefits of holiness. She included fostering intimacy with God, building spiritual strength and stability, making us useful and effective for God's purpose, as well as protecting us and making us productive.

Musawenkosi Dube, an evangelical preacher, adds to this list: "You get peace beyond description. All good things only come from God, the best of which is being in peace with yourself and God Himself." Like I said, the peace that God gives cannot be put down in black and white, yet I encourage you to work at your relationship with Christ to know what I'm talking about.

Physical healing is one of the key benefits of holiness. If you trust God for your healing and express your trust in Him in every way possible, God is not deaf nor is He blind; He will give you healing. Do note that God chooses the way He wants to heal someone. For some, it might take a couple of years while others receive it instantly. He would do that without consulting anyone.

The ultimate benefit of holiness is God's promise of eternal life. Mathew 5:8 states that "Blessed are the pure in heart, for they shall see God." We must encourage ourselves in the Lord: What does a child of God do when discouragement sets in? What should we do when we feel useless, like a complete failure, and an abandoned project? How should we react when we are rejected by those who once cared?

As believers, this is a question we must sincerely answer. We cannot pay lip service to this question because it is a fact of life. Sooner or later, everyone faces the reality of disappointment. It is good to be prepared so that we are not shaken.

In answering this pertinent question, the Apostle Paul told the Corinthians in his first letter, chapter 10:11, "now, all these things happened to them as examples, and they were written for our admonition."

The classical experience of David also gives us an example of what to do and how to respond.

1. Sam 30: 1-6 says, "And it came to pass when David and his men were come to Ziklag on the third day, that the Amalekites had invaded the south, and Ziklag, and smitten Ziklag, and burned it with fire;

2. And had taken the women captives that were therein: they slew not any, either great or small, but carried them away, and went on their way.

3. So David and his men came to the city, and, behold, it was burned with fire; and their wives, and their sons, and their daughters were taken captives.

4. Then David and the people that were with him lifted up their voice and wept until they had no more power to weep.

5. And David's two wives were taken captives, Ahinoam the Jezreelitess, and Abigail the wife of Nabal the Carmelite.

6. And David was greatly distressed; for the people spake of stoning him, because the soul of all the people was grieved, every man for his sons and for his daughters: but David encouraged himself in the Lord his God."

When David arrived home to meet a heap of smoking ruins. Everything was gone; wives, children, cattle and all their property. What do you do when life falls apart in this manner? There are so many important lessons to learn from this story. One of these lessons is the reaction of the key players to the predicament. The scriptures recorded that the first reaction was weeping and wailing. This is an instinctive reaction for anyone that has lost all. They "lifted their voices and wept, until they had no more power to weep."

Although it is very difficult not to weep at such colossal loss, it is, however, imperative to point out that tears do not move God. What moves God is our confidence in Him. Weeping uncontrollably when bad things happen, could even be an indication that one is lowering the power of God before men.

Another noticeable reaction from the incident is the tendency to blame someone else for our predicament. David's men blamed him as the cause of the loss and they were even on the verge of stoning him. Most of the time, we play the blame game. We do play this game either to justify ourselves or look good to others. Blaming others does not remove one's accountability to God, nor does it solve the problem.

The reaction that is worth emulating from the incident is that of David himself. He could have allowed himself to be crushed and overwhelmed by the distress. He could have gotten bitter and angry at God, like we do most times. He could have lost his faith and never recovered.

He could have just stood there and continue to look hopeless and do nothing. The scriptures however recorded that in spite of David's great distress, "...David encouraged himself in the Lord" (1 Samuel 30:6).

David Wilkerson raises an important observation, "Did all this calamity fall upon David because he was living in sin? Was he running from God? Far from it. If anything, David was running with God, but not understanding why the path led through such hard times."

Today, many Christians wonder why they are going through certain situations even though they are diligently serving God. It would be interesting to weigh the enormity of what they are going through and compare it to that of an anointed man like David, a man after God's heart. David, in the face of such colossal loss and grief, encouraged himself in the Lord.

How do you react to down times in your journey of life? According to Wilkerson, "are you distressed at present, desperately needing a fresh anointing? Reject all satanic lies, put away all despairing feelings -- look up and rejoice -- claim the promises of God's presence and faithfulness -- accept His love -- and be embraced by your loving Lord. That is the word of the Lord to all who seek encouragement -- Be embraced! You are going to recover everything!"

Pastor Mark Roper of First Christ Church in Arkansas listed some steps we should take to encourage ourselves in the Lord. The first step, when the going gets tough, is to get alone with God. There are times when the only way to find the encouragement we need is to get alone and seek the face of God. That is why, for instance, we read of Daniel's upper room. In Daniel 6:10, we read of how Jesus often withdrew himself, and in Luke 5:16 we read of John in the wilderness of Zin where he wrote most of his contribution to the Bible.

Roper puts it this way, "David's aloneness was his first step toward wholeness. There can be great healing in solitude. Jim Elliott, the martyred missionary, once wrote in his journal: "I think the devil has made it his business to monopolize on three elements: noise, hurry, and crowds. Satan is quite aware of the power of silence."

There is a ministry in solitude. A real source of power is to be alone, to be quiet, so you can talk to your God and God can talk to you. David knew that. His Psalms show us that he understood the importance of getting alone with God, whether it is in a cave or on a mountainside.

Another step to encourage oneself is to read the Scriptures. The Bible is full of God's promises for all situations in our lives. From matrimony to career, to finance, health, relationships, you name it. These promises are the reason

Christians are told, “this Book of the Law shall not depart from your mouth, but you shall meditate on it day and night, that you may observe to do according to all that is written in it. For then you will make your way prosperous, and then you will have good success” (Joshua 1:8). This passage is just one of the several promises of God to mankind and especially to believers. The word of God is very useful when faced with the downside of life. Meditate on them and see them rekindle your spirit.

A preacher once said, if you don’t believe 100 percent of what God says, then stop being a Christian. He made this statement because the word of God carries the integrity of God. David was very cognizant of this fact, and he used it elaborately. He used it so much so that God gave him the inspiration to pen some of the words himself. These words of David constitute most of the psalms we read today.

Another great step to encourage oneself is to worship the Lord in songs. Singing songs of worship and praising God in times of distress is a very powerful way to encourage oneself. Songs lift the spirit; they rekindle joy even during agony.

Paul and Silas recognized and effectively used this knowledge when they were imprisoned in Acts 16.

“But at midnight Paul and Silas were praying and singing hymns to God, and the prisoners were listening to them. Suddenly there was a great earthquake so that the foundations of the prison were shaken, and immediately all the doors were opened, and everyone’s chains were loosed.”

It is often said among choristers that if you know how to offer high praises to God, your enemies will be in trouble. Psalm 27:6 vindicates that saying, “and now my head shall be lifted up above my enemies all around me; Therefore I will offer sacrifices of joy in His tabernacle; I will sing, yes, I will sing praises to the Lord.”

We should learn to lift our spirit during discouraging moments with songs. It works.

CHAPTER THREE

The Power of Encouraging Words

In his book *Communication and Media Arts*, Emmanuel Akpan made the statement: "man can not communicate." This statement is very relevant here, and it means that human beings are always communicating, one way or the other. They are communicating verbally or non-verbally.

Non-verbal communication cues are numerous. It can be through the use of signs as in sign language, and it can also be through gestures such as shaking of the head for agreement or disagreement, nodding for affirmation or otherwise, the use of body language, and the use of objects for representing a thought. The cross, for instance, signifies crucifixion; a snake coiled on a stick represents the medical field.

John 1:1 is a powerful revelation to mankind. It states that "in the beginning was the Word, and the Word was with God, and the Word was God." This statement gives credence to the import of communication in the life of all humans. Everyone must communicate either in an interpersonal communication between two persons, which is referred to as a dyad, or between three persons as a triad, or in a small group. People engage in mass communication, usually with the aid of a technological medium.

The question now is since individuals cannot help but communicate, what type of communication situation do we create around us? Put it in another way, what type of message do we send out to our receivers? Is the content of the message capable of lifting someone up, or is it a divisive or polarizing communication that is mean and degrading?

We must be very careful of what we say, always and anywhere. The inherent power that words have makes this carefulness necessary. Words are powerful. They can build or destroy, they can encourage or discourage; words are indeed power influencers.

The Bible gives credence to the power of words in James 3:8 - 10.

"8 For every kind of beasts, and of birds, and of serpents, and of things in the sea, is tamed, and hath been tamed of mankind:8 But the tongue can no man tame; it is an unruly evil, full of deadly poison.9 Therewith bless we God, even the Father; and therewith curse we men, which are made after the similitude of God. 10 Out of the same mouth proceedeth blessing and cursing."

This is why Solomon said:

"A soft answer turns away wrath, but a rash word stirs up anger." Proverbs 15:1-2

Again, extra caution is needed in what we say and how we say it. Also, we must take care with our body language and other nonverbal cues that could be picked up during discussions.

The Scripture above warns us about the tremendous damage that we can do with careless words. We should never underestimate the disastrous effect our words can have on another person. Cary Schmidt says words don't just impact once; they impact over and over. Schmidt, who is pastor of Emmanuel Baptist Church in Newington, Connecticut, adds that "things you say today, write today, post today, will live in the hearts and minds of people for much longer than one will remember saying them."

We have the power to speak life or death to our audience. It can be an individual or a group of people. We can use words to build them up with encouragement or tear them down with defeat. Sometimes, we can wound them very deeply with a negative word. The choice of what we do is ours. This power of choice is the reason we must be very careful with what we say and how we say it.

In classes on communication, students learn how an individual encodes a message internally. He or she then speaks it out to a receiver, who decodes the message and responds. Communication takes place when the information there is an understanding of the message, and there is a shared meaning between the two parties.

From this perspective, the speaker who is also known as the encoder has the responsibility to properly encode the words to use before speaking out. Based on the objective of the communication, the communicator can encode to inform, to educate, to entertain, or to encourage.

We can understand the importance of this discussion from a practical example, which Pastor Patrick Sunstrom of River of Life Community Church in North Dakota gave.

"One time when I was at church, I saw one of the young girls with a blue cowboy hat. It was obviously new, and it had a white feather on it. The first thought that flew into my mind was that it was a little bit gaudy and I felt like saying something like, "Aren't you the little cowgirl today?"

Thankfully, instead of letting those careless words tumble out of my mouth, I thought, "Why don't I say something different? You know, the hat looks nice on her. I should tell her that. So, I did just that. I said, 'That's a very pretty hat you have on.'"

It doesn't seem like a simple phrase like that would have much effect, but you should have seen what happened next. Her countenance visibly changed. It was as if a smile came over her entire body, and you could almost feel her beaming when she answered, "Thanks, my mommy just bought it for me!" I was almost floored. I had just witnessed the incredible power that a simple word of encouragement had on another person, and I realized that I would have blown it had I said the first foolish thing that popped into my head."

This Pastor exercised caution in his choice of words. He resisted the urge to speak off the cuff, which would have been devastating for a young lady adorning a gift from her mother for the first time. Instead, the Pastor drew back and re-coded his message before speaking out. This re-coding paid off because of how happy the young lady was. Imagine how it would have been if the Pastor, of all people in the community, was the one talking down on the lady's precious gift from her mother.

The Pastor concluded his narration this way:

"...in closing, I want to encourage you to use the power of your words to build people up and not tear them down. Say kind things to the people you meet and bring a little piece of the kingdom of heaven into their lives. It won't cost you anything, and it won't take up much of your time, but one small kind little word just might make someone's day a little brighter, and it may plant a seed for the kingdom of God in their hearts."

In his epistle to the Ephesians, the Apostle Paul counseled: "*Let no corrupt communication proceed out of your mouth, but that which is good to the use of edifying, that it may minister grace unto the hearers.*" Ephesians 4:29

In this passage, the Apostle Paul warned believers against corrupt communications. He directed us to choose words that are useful and edifying because filthy and offensive communication are not only poisonous, but they are also infectious. Evil communication shows the heart of the speaker because defilement comes from within and not from outside.

Jesus spoke about communications in Mathew 15:11:

"Not what goes into the mouth defiles a man, but what comes out of the mouth, this defiles a man."

The disciples were told they do not defile themselves by what they eat, but with what they speak out with spite. It is explicitly clear that we are polluted, more importantly by the words we speak from an unsanctified heart. What we eat or dirty hands are not as critical as what we imbibe through thoughts and exhale through unholy words. Christians should not only put off corrupt communication from our mouth, but, as the verse instructed, we must say that which is good to the use of edifying. Encouraging words are powerful, and they do make the difference.

Miguel Angel says:

"Be impeccable with your word. Speak with integrity. Say only what you mean. Avoid using the word to speak against yourself or to gossip about others. Use the power of your word in the direction of truth and love."

We must realize that our words can minister grace and gladness and help the discouraged or the depressed heart.

King Solomon has this to say in Proverbs 12:25:

"Anxiety in the heart of a man causes depression, but a good word makes it glad."

As part of the recommendations to overcome depression, The Redeemed Christian Church of God's Sunday School

Manual for 2016 listed the need to, "initiate communication with pastors, friends, and trusted family members for counseling. Avoid isolation and talk." Indeed, a well-encoded and well-delivered word that is timely can make a heavy heart or a depressed heart glad. This is what Proverbs 16:24 says:

"Pleasant words are like a honeycomb, sweetness to the soul and health to the bones."

This is the practical reason why some people would make sure they attend church services, because besides not forsaking the gathering of the saints as stated in Hebrews 10:25, they also attend church service, believing in God for a word of encouragement concerning their situation.

When the word of God ministers to our circumstances, it makes the difference. A young man once attended a special service with the desire that God should increase his height. During the service, the man of God as led by the spirit of God delivered a word of prophecy that God says He is increasing the height of someone in the congregation.

At the end of the service, the young man whose desire was an increase in height, noticed that both his shirts and trousers had become shorter for his height, an indication that the spoken word from the man of God has ministered to his special circumstance.

As chronicled by the Redemption Light, a monthly publication of the Redeemed Christian Church of God, (Vol. 18. No. 07), Pastor and Mrs. Soji Oni, after their wedding, had a delay of 23 years before they could get a child. While at the Redemption Camp for one of the Holy Ghost services, someone gave a testimony about God blessing her family with a set of twins; afterward, the General Overseer, Pastor Enoch Adeboye, gave a word of prophecy that "someone was telling God in his heart that I'm not even asking for twins, just give me one, God said you will have three."

The husband narrated that, "my wife keyed into the prophecy

and when the service was over, she told me that the prophecy was for us and it was as if the Pastor saw what was in our minds. A few months later, my wife became pregnant, and when she went for a scan, the doctors were afraid when the scan revealed that she had three children in her womb. They were afraid because of her age, she was close to 50 years then. According to the doctors, multiple pregnancies for young ladies could be very challenging, not to mention a woman of her age. Eventually, God blessed us with a set of triplets on December 21, 2012, and because of their number, they were very small. They weighed 1.65kg, 1.15 kg, and 1.2 kg respectively and had to be put in the incubator."

This is a typical instance of believing God for a word of comfort concerning one's situation, and it worked out for the erstwhile barren couple. It is a good example of the power of words to encourage and strengthen, just what Solomon meant when he said in Songs of Solomon 4:11, "honey and milk are under your tongue."

We must, therefore, follow God's example and speak encouraging words at any point and time.

"For everything that was written in the past was written to teach us, so that through endurance and the encouragement of the Scriptures we might have hope." Romans 15:4

How to appropriate the power of encouraging words: The scriptures instruct believers to encourage one another.

"Therefore encourage one another and build each other up, just as in fact you are doing." 1 Thessalonians 5:11

The apostles did it: "Judas and Silas, who themselves were prophets, said much to encourage and strengthen the brothers" (Acts 15:32), therefore, we must also do it deliberately and continuously. Tony Robbins once said, "it is not what we do once in a while that shapes our lives, but what we do consistently."

A good way to stay encouraged and to be an encourager is to stay positive yourself. This may sound simplistic. When we acknowledge that life could be very unkind, and that life is full of assorted challenges; staying positive or encoding positive words to encourage the next person, could be a daunting task. We must focus on the sunny side of life to be able to speak words of encouragement to others.

Let us learn from Thomas Edison who experienced so many failures before he could make a breakthrough with inventing the light bulb. He said:

"Our greatest weakness lies in giving up. The most certain way to succeed is always to try just one more time."

We can use both verbal and written words to encourage, although the impact works differently. I was looking for something very different the other day and came across a note that a sister in the church, who is named Laurel, whom the Lord used me to the disciple, sent to me when I was relocating from my country some years back. Seven years later, as I again went through the note, it was accompanied by a book gift titled *Getting Through What You're Going Through*, by Robert Schuller.

I was freshly overwhelmed with joy and gratitude and guess what, I even tried to keep the three short paragraphs note even safer. I hope to meet her one day to thank her again for her thoughtfulness. It was very encouraging to me because at that time, I was considered too strict by both adults and youth that I disciple. This did not bother me anyway, but for one of them to consider writing such beautiful words of how I led her to Christ, I was overwhelmed with joy and appreciation.

Since scriptures tell us that it is what comes out that defiles an individual, we must, therefore, think positively before we speak out. Doug Britton points out that, "When you talk, you make a series of choices about what subjects to discuss, what memories to bring up, and what points to make. There always are negative things you could say, but there also are positive ones. Choose the positive. Choose to specialize in encouraging words, not in critical comments," the Bible says:

"Let us, therefore, make every effort to do what leads to peace and to mutual edification." Romans 14:19

Doug, in his teaching on the power of encouraging words, listed the following points as practical ways to be an encourager:

Bring friendly speech into your relationships.

Don't start complaining as soon as you see your spouse, child, employee, neighbor, or someone else. Ask about his or her day. Give a compliment. Share stories about your day, insights from a Bible study, victories on the job, or other things they may be interested in.

Voice words of encouragement, appreciation, support, and respect.

Acknowledge the other person's' abilities and efforts. If someone feels inadequate, encourage him or her.

Monitor your positive and negative remarks.

Learn to be self-aware and listen to what you say. Be sure you make positive comments and not negative ones.

Respond to problems with hope and encouragement.

When someone talks about personal difficulties, do not respond with a "gloom and doom" attitude. Listen with compassion and avoid simplistic advice. Say something such as, "I know this is a tough time for you, but it won't last. Let me encourage you: God will see you through, and I'm here to help, too."

'God comforts us in all our troubles, so that we can comfort those in any trouble with the comfort we ourselves have received from God." 2 Corinthians 1:4

In the same vein, the Apostle Paul counseled, "We urge you, brothers, warn those who are idle, encourage the timid, help the weak, be patient with everyone." 1 Thessalonians 5:14

Avoid subtle criticisms.

Watch out for subtle ways you may tear others down, such as pointing out how quickly you can mow the lawn when you know it takes them twice as long.

Discuss problems with a friend.

There are times in every relationship—in a family, on the job, or wherever—when people discuss difficult topics. When you do, speak in a courteous, friendly manner. The way you speak usually is more important than whether your opinions are right or wrong.

In addition to the above, Nancy DeMoss, in her series of power of encouraging words, discusses tools that could be useful in sending out words of encouragement. According to her:

"I have found that voicemail can be a real great means of encouraging people. I've had somebody call my voicemail and pray a prayer for me on that voicemail or speak words of encouragement. "I know you're recording for *Revive Our Hearts* today." I'll often get that kind of voicemail. "And I just want you to know that I'm thinking about you, that I'm praying for you."

We can use the phone to speak words of encouragement. I made a call not too long ago to a woman that I had never even met, but her husband works with one of our partner ministries. I knew that his dad was hospitalized with a very serious illness and he had to be out of town caring for his dad. This wife had a newborn baby and a couple of little children in addition to the baby.

DeMoss-Wooglemuth went further to advise us to use the telephone to speak words of encouragement efficiently. She described a situation in which she called a woman whose husband works with a partner ministry. She called to bless the family in the middle of intense stress. Nancy had this to say: "Her name just crossed my heart one day. I don't know her, but I picked up the phone, and I said, "Carrie. I just want you to know that I've been thinking about you... I just wanted to call and tell you that I'm thinking about you and I want to pray for you." God used these encouraging words in ways that Nancy could never have imagined.

Writing both long and short notes to those who are precious to us is another way to be an encourager. I write continuously to Pastors and other ministers in the Redeemed Christian Church of God, and other associated ministries. We write and send a Card with gifts to every Pastor on their Birthdays and other significant events. We are grateful to God for the incredible response that we get through this simple ministry. Writing is an ancient art that the Apostles practiced in their time. The long list of letters that forms our present day Bible are relational books. It is also important to note that virtually all the prophetic messages are targeted writings. We need to copy this great habit of the Apostles and the Prophets.

Nancy Demoss Wooglemoth has this to say: "I got an email from one of my precious praying friends this past week. She said, "My dear friend. It's 2 a.m. and you are heavy on my heart and in my prayers. Because you are on the front lines, I just wanted you to know you have someone lifting your arms up in the battle and that the midnight oil has been burning for you in prayers while you sleep because you are a precious friend and you are precious in the sight of the Lord. Love, prayers and blessings, Susan." "I didn't get that until the next day. But even now I think about that friend Susan and my heart is encouraged and strengthened in the Lord. There is such power through the written word."

Everyone can be an encourager by giving the gift of Scriptures that touch our hearts. In our moments of study, when we are exposed to messages, as we meditate on God's word;

thoughts will come to us. Let us write down these ideas, make them into simple but beautiful table piece, bookmark, etc., and give to people that we want to encourage. Imagine how this Scripture carefully printed on a picturesque background and framed will look in the Office or on the table of one of your sisters or brothers, imagine!

"For the LORD God is a sun and shield: the LORD will give grace and glory: no good thing will he withhold from them that walk uprightly.

This Scripture is Psalm 84:11. It is a powerful word that will bring hope and encouragement to someone. There are many encouraging passages in the Scriptures. We can use these Scriptures – today, to be an encourager.

I know someone who lives by sharing encouraging Scriptures. He cannot speak ten words but that he will use a Scripture that encourages his listener. Whether on the phone, in writing or one on one, this brother is overflowing with encouraging words. So many families and distressed individuals receive encouragement from this brother who joyfully shares God's word. There is nothing that stops any of us from bringing this form of encouragement to God's people.

Do think about this possibility. You find three Scriptures a week and use each of the Scriptures to encourage four people. Before the end of the week, you will have been a blessing to twelve individuals! God's love will flow like a river through us; God will bless many souls, and there will be great rejoicing in heaven because of the simple but strategic gift of Scriptures.

Motivational Speeches: The efficacy of words in encouragement, healing, education, and information , gave rise to motivational talks and speeches. This is because motivational speeches thrive in power behind words to inspire, motivate, encourage, and meet needs.

Skill in motivational speeches did not just start; they emanate from Bible where we have great speeches to motivate the Israelites to worship and serve God, as in the example of the great valedictory speech of Moses that constitutes the entire book of Deuteronomy, those given by a host of other prophets, and those given by the disciples and Jesus Christ himself as inspired by the Holy Spirit. In both speech and action, the word of God is powerful, for by it, God created all things, and by it, he still cares for his people.

The word of God has the power to create, Psalm 33:6, power to sustain all creation, Hebrews 1:3, power to heal, Psalm 107:20, power to judge our hearts, Hebrews 4:12, and power to lead us to faith, Romans 10:17. The word of God also has the power to save us, 2 Timothy 3:15, power to make us holy, Ephesians 5:26, power to fight against Satan, Ephesians 6:17, as well as power to destroy the world, 2 Peter 3:7, all because of its characteristic nature of integrity and reliability, 2 Samuel 7:28, flawlessness, Proverbs 30:5, alive and active, Hebrews 4:12 and most importantly its always the truth, John 17:17, 1 Kings 17:24.

However, although everyone is made by God, not everyone is of God, but everyone uses words to communicate. As pointed out earlier, man can not communicate. Some people even speak for a living, paid to speak on their professional skills, others to teach, and many others to create fun like stand-up comedians and masters of ceremony.

In all these speech-centered trades, the key element is the use of words to communicate whatever is required from them, and this is where the skill to use power words to achieve that motive comes, and herein lays motivational speeches.

As the name implies, motivational speeches are speeches given to move people to action or cause something to happen, drive, prod and prompt. At the heart of motivational speech is usually a story of endurance, patience, and achievement.

Motivational speeches are intended to lift hearts in dark times, inspire brave feats, give courage to the weary, honor the dead, encourage the living, and ultimately change the course of history.

All these cannot be achieved if the choice of words is weak. Brett and Kate MacKay note that great oratory has three components: style, substance, and impact.

In terms of style, they stated that, "a great speech must be masterfully constructed as the best orators are masters of both written and spoken word, and use words to create texts that are beautiful to both hear and read."

"Speech," the Mackays indicated, "may be flowery and charismatically presented and yet lack any true substance at all. Great speeches must center on a worthy theme; it must appeal to and inspire the audience's finest values and ideals."

In terms of impact, they reasoned that it must be persuasive and "the very best speeches change hearts and minds and seem as revelatory several decades or centuries removed as when they were first given."

Throughout the course of world history, great speeches have influenced and changed the trajectory of our past. From that of Moses to both Pharaoh and the Israelites, to Jesus Christ's Sermon on the Mount, to the inaugural speeches of modern leaders, their words have become an inspiration to millions of people, especially in their darkest hours.

Therefore, if a man wishes to effectively use the power of encouraging words, he must first emulate the life and style of those before him. He must immerse himself not only in their texts, but also in their values, especially that of the selfless Jesus Christ, whose sermons are as active and living today as they were over 2000 years ago.

In this direction, therefore, this chapter would end with some of these encouraging motivational words to help us replace negative thoughts with inspiring words and ideas.

Scriptural Quotes for Encouragement

The Bible is full of strength scriptures to live by. These passages will bring many encouraging thoughts to your day.

Deuteronomy 31:6 - Be strong and courageous. Do not fear or be in dread of them, for it is the LORD your God who goes with you. He will not leave you or forsake you."

Isaiah 41:10 - Fear not, for I am with you; be not dismayed, for I am your God; I will strengthen you, I will help you, I will uphold you with my righteous right hand.

Zephaniah 3:17 - The LORD your God is in your midst, a mighty one who will save; he will rejoice over you with gladness; he will quiet you by his love; he will exult over you with loud singing.

1 Corinthians 10:13 - No temptation has overtaken you that is not common to man. God is faithful, and he will not let you be tempted beyond your ability, but with the temptation he will also provide the way of escape, that you may be able to endure it.

2 Corinthians 4:16-18 - So we do not lose heart. Though our outer self is wasting away, our inner self is being renewed day by day. For this light momentary affliction is preparing for us an eternal weight of glory beyond all comparison, as we look not to the things that are seen but to the things that are unseen. For the things that are seen are transient, but the things that are unseen are eternal.

Bible Verses for Comfort and Encouragement

There are times in everyone's life when we need encouragement and comfort. The Bible is great for this type of need also.

Deuteronomy 31:8 - It is the LORD who goes before you. He will be with you; he will not leave you or forsake you. Do not fear or be dismayed.

Psalm 9:9 - The LORD is a stronghold for the oppressed, a stronghold in times of trouble. And those who know your name put their trust in you, for you, O LORD, have not forsaken those who seek you.

Psalm 23:4 - Even though I walk through the valley of the shadow of death, I will fear no evil, for you are with me; your rod and your staff, they comfort me.

Psalm 55:22 - Cast your burden on the LORD, and he will sustain you; he will never permit the righteous to be moved.

Matthew 11:28-29 - Come to me, all who labor and arc heavy laden, and I will give you rest. Take my yoke upon you, and learn from me, for I am gentle and lowly in heart, and you will find rest for your souls.

Scripture Quotes for Peace and Encouragement

How great is it to open the Bible and read words from the Prince of Peace giving us quotes to live by.

John 14:27 - Peace I leave with you; my peace I give to you. Not as the world gives do I give to you. Let not your hearts be troubled, neither let them be afraid.

John 16:33 - I have said these things to you, that in me you may have peace. In the world, you will have tribulation. But take heart; I have overcome the world."

Romans 8:6 - For to set the mind on the flesh is death, but to set the mind on the Spirit is life and peace.

Philippians 4:6-7 - Do not be anxious about anything, but in everything by prayer and supplication with thanksgiving let your requests be made known to God. And the peace of God, which surpasses all understanding, will guard your hearts and your minds in Christ Jesus.

Colossians 3:15 - And let the peace of Christ rule in your hearts, to which indeed you were called in one body. And be thankful.

Encouragement through God's Promises

The promises that come in God's word are sure to encourage you in your walk with Christ today.

The Promise of Eternal Life

John 6:47 - Truly, truly, I say to you, whoever believes has eternal life.

God is Faithful

Deuteronomy 7:9 - Know therefore that the LORD your God is God, the faithful God who keeps covenant and steadfast love with those who love him and keep his commandments, to a thousand generations

God Promises to Guide Us

Psalm 32:8 - I will instruct you and teach you in the way you should go; I will counsel you with my eye upon you.

2 Timothy 3:16-17 - All Scripture is breathed out by God and profitable for teaching, for reproof, for correction, and for training in righteousness, that the man of God may be competent, equipped for every good work.

God Hears Our Prayers

1 John 5:14 - And this is the confidence that we have toward him, that if we ask anything according to his will, he hears us.

Some Christian Encouragement Quotes

God will not be absent when His people are on trial; he will stand in court as their advocate, to plead on their behalf.

Charles Haddon Spurgeon

You are valuable because you exist. Not because of what you do or what you have done, but simply because you are.

Max Lucado

Be assured, if you walk with Him and look to Him, and expect help from Him, He will never fail you.

George Mueller

The stars may fall, but God's promises will stand and be fulfilled.

J. I. Packer

Apart from the scriptures, there are also some encouraging philosophical quotes by great orators in history. Some of them are reproduced here to encourage us:

Words of Encouragement
When Life's Getting You Down

"When you get into a tight place and everything goes against you, till it seems as though you could not hang on a minute longer, never give up then, for that is just the place and time that the tide will turn"

Harriet Beecher Stowe

"I'm not saying everything is survivable. Just that everything except the last thing is."

John Green in his book, Paper Towns

"A diamond is a piece of charcoal that handled stress exceptionally well."

Unknown

"The earth has music for those who listen."

Shakespeare

"I took a deep breath and listened to the bray of my heart. I am. I am. I am."

Sylvia Plath

"Think of all the beauty still left around you and be happy."

Anne Frank

"One day, in retrospect, the years of struggle will strike you as the most beautiful."

Sigmund Freud

"As I look back on my life, I realize that every time I thought I was being rejected from something good, I was actually being directed to something better."

Dr. Steve Marboli

"A smooth sea never made a skilled sailor."

English Proverb

"Success is the ability to go from one failure to another with no loss of enthusiasm."

Winston Churchill

Words for When Others Are Getting You Down

"People will kill you over time, and how they'll kill you is with tiny, harmless phrases, like "be realistic."

Dylan Moran

"Once in a while, it really hits people that they don't have to experience the world in the way they have been told to."

Alan Keightley

"Do not feel lonely; the entire universe is inside you."

Philosopher Rumi

"If you are always trying to be normal, you will never know how amazing you can be."

Maya Angelou

"There wouldn't be a sky full of stars if we were all meant to wish on the same one."

Frances Clark

"When you do something beautiful and nobody notices, do not be sad. For the sun every morning is a beautiful spectacle and yet most of the audience still sleeps."

John Lennon

"As people grow up, they realize it's less important to have more friends and more important to have real ones."

Lauren Conrad

"The question isn't who is going to let me; it's who is going to stop me."

Ayn Rand

Words When You Need Inspiration

"Respond to every call that excites your spirit." ~

Rumi

"Your work is to discover your work and then, with all your heart, give yourself to it."

Buddha

"I still find each day too short for all the thoughts I want to think, all the walks I want to take, all the books I want to read, and all the friends I want to see."

John Burroughs

"We keep moving forward, opening new doors and doing new things, because we're curious, and curiosity keeps leading us down new paths."

Walt Disney

"Let yourself be silently drawn by the strange pull of what you really love. It will not lead you astray."

Rumi

"I'm a slow walker, but I never walk back."

Abraham Lincoln

"Creativity is intelligence having fun."

Albert Einstein

"People often say that motivation doesn't last. Well, neither does bathing. That's why we recommend it daily."

Zig Ziglar

"You create your thoughts, your thoughts create your intentions, and your intentions create your reality."

Wayne Dyer

"If you can't figure out your purpose, find out your passion. For your passion will lead you right into your purpose."

T.D. Jakes

Words of Encouragement When You're Doubting Yourself or Your Choices

"The what-if's and the should-have's will eat your brain."

John O'Callaghan

"And now that you don't have to be perfect, you can be good."

John Steinbeck

"Never lose sight of the fact that just being is fun."

Katharine Hepburn

"You have to leave the city of your comfort and go into the wilderness of your intuition."

Alan Alda

"It's impossible,' said pride. 'It's risky,' said experience. 'It's pointless,' said reason. 'Give it a try,' whispered the heart."

Unknown

"Believe in yourself and all that you are. Know that there is something inside you that is greater than any obstacle."

Christian D. Larson

"Change can be scary, but you know what's scarier? Allowing fear to stop you from growing, evolving, and progressing."

Mandy Hale

"Courage does not always roar. Sometimes courage is the quiet voice at the end of the day saying, 'I will try again tomorrow.'"

Mary Anne Radmacher

"I am always doing what I can't do so I may learn how to do it."

Vincent Van Gogh

"Never give up on a dream just because of the time it will take to accomplish it. The time will pass anyway."

Earl Nightingale

"A ship is always safe at shore, but that's not what it's built for."

Albert Einstein

CHAPTER FOUR

Sources of Encouragement

Do you feel the candle of your dream is fading? Maybe due to unforeseen challenges, you are afraid of what the outcome of an investigation would be, or you are worried about the result of the lab test or your career and relationship? Remember that no one is immune to problems; even the lion must fight off flies.

There is good news, however. Amid these challenges, there is the prospect for growth. Oscar Wilde once observed, "What seems to us bitter trials are often blessings in disguise." When you trust God's sovereignty, opportunities may come wrapped as obstacles.

There is a fact of life, and it is this: if you find a path with no obstacles, it is most likely a path that leads to nowhere important because nothing good comes easy. Adversity is often the mother of invention. Great testimonies have shown that man's adversity is always God's opportunity.

Your struggle may be lasting, but it will not be everlasting. That is why the Apostle Paul offered these words of encouragement in 2 Corinthians 4:8-9:

"We are hard pressed on every side, but not crushed; perplexed, but not in despair; persecuted, but not abandoned; struck down, but not destroyed."

John Mason sees it this way:

"Your life will be much more productive if you understand that obstacles are part of life; and if you want your place in the sun, you will have to expect some blisters."

The scriptures couldn't have been more inspiring when it warned in the Old Testament that:

"Man who is born of woman is of few days and full of trouble." Job 14:1

During the days of Christ, the New Testament comforts us this way: *"I have told you these things, so that in me you may have peace. In this world, you will have trouble. But take heart! I have overcome the world."* John 16:33

Do you suddenly start facing some unexplainable challenges at work or home, in your career, with your finances, or in relationships? How do you respond to the situation? Did you throw in the towel and quit the job? Did you file for divorce or file for bankruptcy? Each of us must ask ourselves where is our trust in God and where is the Eagle in us? When you determine not to give up, God offers you the strength to soar above life's test and trials.

"But those who wait on the Lord shall renew their strength; they shall mount up with wings like eagles, they shall run and not be weary, they shall walk and not faint." Isaiah 40:31

Like the Eagle, when you don't give up, you increase your determination to succeed, and by so doing you will turn adversaries and challenges into opportunities.

Barry Black, while writing the final words in his book, *The Blessings of Adversity*, says, "When trouble comes, look for God's blessings in your adversity. He is in the business of growing believers who can withstand life's storms."

Take an example from the list below of people like you and me who turned their adversity to blessings:

Henry Ford, who invented cars, went broke five times before he succeeded.

A newspaper fired **Walt Disney** for lack of ideas, but he left to build Disneyland, the world leading resort center today.

Oprah Winfrey was fired from WJTV for inability to broadcast. Today she is the richest Black American woman, worth over $3 billion from television broadcasting.

A voice teacher said **Enrico Caruso** had no future in music, his parents believed, but he did not accept what the teacher said and worked to become one of the most famous opera singers in the world.

Theodore Roosevelt suffered the deaths of his mother and his wife on the same day in 1884 before he became a war hero, and later the President of United States.

John Wesley was often asked not to return to churches after preaching to them once. When he preached in a meadow, people turned a bull loose on him. He later founded the Methodist Church.

Albert Einstein didn't speak until he was four years old and didn't read until age seven, was expelled from school, refused admission to others, but eventually became a pillar of modern physics.

Thomas Edison's teachers said he was, "too stupid to learn anything," he was fired from his first two jobs, made 1000 unsuccessful attempts at inventing the light bulb, but eventually invented the bulb.

Muhammed Buhari contested for President of his country and failed three times. He eventually won the presidency after 12 years of failure.

One thing common with all these people is that they did not give up; the scripture says:

"For a great door and effectual is opened unto me, and there are many adversaries." 1 Corinthians 16:9

So again, when an inevitable challenge faces you, how do you respond?

Nehemiah could have abandoned the building of the wall because he faced several challenges, opposition, and mockery.

"And all of them conspired together to come and attack Jerusalem and create confusion. Nevertheless we made our prayer to our God, and because of them we set a watch against them day and night." Nehemiah 4:8-9

Rather than abandon the Wall, Nehemiah mobilized the people to watch and pray when he was faced with a discouraging situation. So, here comes the very first source of encouragement: **prayer.**

Bishop T.D. Jakes refers to prayer as a "spiritual software update." Speaking to *Simple Grace* magazine, he says: "Prayer is critical because it gets down to our cores, it acknowledges our limitations and it recognizes that God understands the things we haven't figured out yet, so it's like if you have a problem with your computer, you want to take it to the company that made it. Similarly, if you have trouble with your life, you want to go to God who gave it."

The Potter's House Bishop went on: "I have a quiet place in my home that I do this spiritual software update, I start my day there, and when something's troubling me I go there, but I also pray as I go about my day, truth is sometimes I have no one else to talk to but God. Either someone has confided a secret in me, or there's a problem that I need to bring to God first. But He is always there, listening and loving."

When things hoped for are yet to happen, wise people respond by crying unto their God (Psalm 121:1, Psalm 142, and Psalm 120); they don't wallow in self-pity, shedding tears, because as pointed out in previous chapter, our confidence in Him and not tears, is what moves God.

When you cry unto Him with a humble heart, God remembers His promises (John 10:10, Deuteronomy. 1:8) and when God remembers His promises, He arises for your sake (Isaiah 28:21, Psalm 68). Come to think of it, compared to the huge monthly bills we pay to telephone companies for our telephone calls, we have a free and direct access to God through our prayers.

Robert Schuller in his book, *Getting Through What You' re Going Through,* calls this a good news, which indeed it is. Hear him:

"The good news for those of us going through a difficult time is that we have a hotline to God. And guess what? It doesn't even cost a dime, it's free."

Schuller calls prayer during distress, prayer of petition. It is interesting to note that since Adam told God:

"The woman whom you gave to be with me, she gave me of the tree, and I ate," Genesis 3:12

God now expects us to ask Him for our wants and needs. (Mathew 7:7) In the parable of the persistent woman and the judge in Luke 18, Jesus encourages that we "always ought to pray and not lose heart."

The account has it that this woman, a widow, went to the judge to ask him to avenge a wrong that had been committed against her. The first time the woman went to the judge, her request was denied; she was turned away.

Each time she went back to the judge, she was denied justice, but she was not deterred as she kept going back until finally, the judge reasoned that the only way he would stop the woman from coming again, was to give her what she was asking for.

Fresh insights from this parable as put forth by Schuller are worth noting:

"This woman came to an unjust judge, we come to a righteous father. This woman had no one to speak for her, we have an advocate before the father, His own son, Jesus Christ, our intercessor. This woman was not invited to speak to the judge, we are allowed to ask and we are promised that our needs will be met."

I sensed somebody thinking aloud, "But Pastor, it seems that the more I pray, the worse things become." Yes, it does happen, but remember that the greatest difficulty always comes right before the birth of a dream. It is always darkest right before dawn. What you may not know is that, you are closer to your miracle than you think; it will happen suddenly. Peter was washing his net to end an unsuccessful fishing night, but right then, it happened, he caught more than ever anticipated (Luke 5).

When God arises for His people, He does not work like an engineer with so many specifications and analyses, or like a doctor with all the appointments, diagnoses, lab tests, and dispensary. When God arises for His own, things begin to happen suddenly, immediately, and at once as in Psalm 126.

Remember that God does not pay by the seconds, like we pay our service providers. He pays at the end, a reason the laborers hired from the market place were all paid "when evening had come" (Mathew 20:8).

A consistent prayer of petition, a prayer that returns God's words to Him in prayers, can encourage the faint hearted, thus introducing another source of encouragement: use of God's words.

Without necessarily repeating what we shared in the

last chapter on the power of encouraging words, the efficacy of God's words in the life of a believer cannot be overemphasized.

David, for instance, devoted a greater portion of Psalm 119, his longest Psalm, to extol the excellences of the word to comfort, counsel, direct, and guide.

He opens the Psalm by telling us the secret of happy living—those who keep the words of God. To achieve this glorious state, he counseled in verse 11, "Your word I have hidden in my heart, that I might not sin against You."

Extolling the usefulness of the word in encouragement, he specifically said in verse 50, "This is my comfort in my affliction, for Your word has given me life."

It is on record that although David was anointed at an early age, not many people then and now have faced the type of afflictions David encountered even after the anointing. In all that he went through, however, you can imagine his faith talk in verse 71:

"It is good for me that I have been afflicted, that I may learn Your statutes."

David gave credence to what the Apostle Paul said in his practical exhortation in Romans 5:3:

"...but we also glory in tribulations, knowing that tribulation produces perseverance, and perseverance, character and character, hope."

Generally, Psalm 119 is a place Christians need to visit often to encourage themselves with the word. Among other things, it is the declaration of the mind of God, His judgment, His righteousness, truth, and above all, His faithfulness.

Prophet Isaiah confirms the trust in God's words:

"So shall My word be that goes forth from My mouth; it shall not return to Me void, but it shall accomplish what I please, and it shall prosper in the thing for which I sent it." Isaiah 55:11

God's words are love letters from Him to encourage us. John 1:3 tells us that Jesus is the creative word and we must treat the word with respect. One way of treating God's words with the needed respect is to meditate on it day and night and to act upon them knowing that one of God's primary ways of bringing about healing and breakthrough is through the power of his word.

Consider for instance a word like in Isaiah 51:3 that says, "For the Lord will comfort Zion, He will comfort all her waste places; He will make her wilderness like Eden, And her desert like the garden of the Lord; Joy and gladness will be found in it, Thanksgiving and the voice of melody."

God's word is active and encourages us in several ways. Let your afflictions lead you to God's words. Devour the scriptures, memorize them, and use them to receive divine encouragement.

We can also encourage ourselves with songs of praises. A combination of prayers, words, and songs of praises is an effective source of encouragement. The talk of encouragement arises when things are not going the way we want it. Disappointments, failures, unmet needs, emotionally crushed, fear, betrayal, delay, abuse, guilt, persecution, anger, unloved, lonely – these are all things to bring to God.

In such situations, we must follow the biblical tradition as pioneered by David who said, "I will bless the Lord at all times; His praise shall continually be in my mouth. My soul shall make its boast in the Lord; The humble shall hear of it and be glad. Oh, magnify the Lord with me, and let us exalt His name together." Psalm 34:1-3

The amazing thing about this very Psalm is that David wrote it when he was under intense persecution that he even pretended madness before Abimelech, who drove him away. This was a very disturbing moment of his life, that would make most of us question God, but that was not for David; instead he was busy praising God.

The Bible is replete with instances of David praising God and not just alone, but also enjoining his followers and by extension, enjoining us, to praise God. 1 Chronicles 29:20, is an example of David urging the whole assembly to:

"...give praise to the Lord your God."

We have a mandatory duty to praise God in good times, and even more so in trying times because God commands it (Joel 2:26, Ephesians 1:3, 1 Thessalonians 5:18).

It might interest you to know that praising God is a command. It is an important element of Christian prayer to focus our attention on God and tell Him how awed we are at his majesty and glory.

This focus was exemplified by Paul and Silas in Acts 16. Paul and Silas were in a grave situation, and they did not give up. Rather, they encouraged themselves in the Lord. They did so with praises, and it paid off for them. It would pay off for you also, as you subscribe to praising God always, regardless of the circumstances.

Barry Black captures it this way: "It is no accident that when Paul and Silas experienced the affliction of an unjust incarceration, they not only found comfort in singing, but they used praise to invite heaven's help. Their praise triggered the earthquake that freed them and brought spiritual liberation to their warden and family."

You too will receive such liberation in Jesus name.

I have never stopped recounting an experience that I had several years ago at a burial ceremony I attended. One of the children of the deceased was saying thank you Jesus all through the event and I was wondering why she should be thanking God instead of crying like the rest of the people were doing; but, I now understand better.

Today, let us learn from these examples and encourage ourselves by praising God, in our own way. In the midst of whatever you are going through, drop them at Jesus' feet and praise Him with all your strength and heart.

Do not allow the devil to steal our joy in the Lord because the moment he steals our joy, we are first discouraged, if care is not taken we become depressed, and then, we are ultimately defeated. This process is the sole aim of the devil but we cannot give in. Let us make the joy of the Lord our strength (Nehemiah 8:10). We must not lose joy.

We can maintain our joy in the Lord through praise and worship. When we do this, we invite God's presence as Paul and Silas did.

We must praise God always, not only when we are in church. People who only praise God on weekends are several days tardy. Praising God, always and daily, allows His presence to abide with us; and that brings us to yet another great source of encouragement: **His presence.**

When an individual in a frustrating situation embarks on prayers of petition, employing the words of God, empowered with a good dose of praise and worship, it only follows suit that the presence of God comes down and takes away all sorrows and gnashing of teeth. We can thus add here that God's Presence is a good source of encouragement.

Without a doubt, the greatest encouragement is that from God. Accepted that we can neither see nor touch God, but we can feel His presence. Robert Schuller explains that, "God comforts us during the difficult times if we confess our problems and just say, comfort me, Lord."

This counsel may sound commonplace, but we need to remember that some people could be so bitter about their struggles that instead of turning to God when faced with situations, they turn away from Him. Others don't even admit they need help. Therefore, the song writer, Joseph Scriven wrote, "Have we trials and temptations! Take it to the Lord in prayers."

On an occasion when Joseph became ill far from home, a friend who was visiting with him discovered a poem near his bed and asked who had written it. Scriven said, "The Lord and I did it between us." He thought the poem, which eventually became a hit hymn, would perhaps, bring some spiritual comfort to his Mom, who still lived in Ireland.

One way to get encouragement through the presence of God is having a repentant and broken spirit, as demonstrated by David in Psalm 51. This most eminent of the penitential psalms depicts the most expressive desires of a repenting sinner.

In the Psalm, David makes heart-felt confessions and seeks peace with his conscience (verses 3-6). In verse 8, he expresses the pain of a heart that is truly broken for sin. He compared the pains to that of a broken bone. As a panacea for peace of mind and comfort, David prayed for a complete pardon.

Despite the apparent discipline through the death of the son who was born out of David's sin (2 Samuel 12), David was still confident that God in His infinite mercies could rekindle his joy. Unfortunately, most people will go into such brokenness today only when they have lost expensive material things or there is the death of a dear one and definitely not when they have committed a sin. People now sin with impunity.

To achieve David's kind of brokenness, which endeared him into God and made him the person after God's heart, we must admit our failings. This admission will enable us to confess and refrain from our sins. It is admission that propels confession (Psalm 32:5, 1 John 1:9).

We must also receive and endure discipline, especially that done out of love and meant for growth and betterment of the recipient (Proverbs 3:12, Revelations 3:19).

Incidentally, today, discipline is rebuffed even by some Christians (Proverbs 17:10). We now relegate discipline to something meted out to children. To achieve brokenness, we must align ourselves with the will of God by inquiring from God all our steps before we take them (1 Chronicles 15:13). We must submit to the discipline and be led by the Spirit of God.

Trusting God's sovereignty can empower us to find joy, even in suffering and during setbacks. When we add a forgiving heart and living a holy life to this list, then we can be expectant of His presence.

Pastor Enoch Adeboye explains it this way:

"When you are born again, you have the presence of God inside of you in some measure. But as you cultivate His friendship, relate with Him daily, praise and worship Him, feed on His word and obey Him, that presence grows."

Adeboye added:

"You need the presence of God to deal with enemies and every situation or challenge that comes your way. The problems you can solve will be determined by the amount of God's presence upon you."

His presence takes away hindrances to progress. He turns disappointment into appointment, and brings about fruitfulness as we can see in the life and family of Obededom. 1 Chronicles 26:4-8. God's presence turned his children into mighty men of valor above all discouraging situations.

Having considered some divine sources of encouragement, we can also take a quick look at what fellow human beings can do to encourage one another.

The instruction in 1 Thessalonians 5:11 gives us all the assignment of encouragement:

"Therefore encourage one another and build each other up, just as in fact you are doing."

Spouses, parents, children, prophets, preachers' friends,

family, and associates all have definite roles as sources of encouragement.

Whether it is in the spiritual sphere or in the secular sphere, we are duty bound to encourage each other. Without encouragement, hardship and frustration thrive and weaken our willpower to get anything done. We do need each other and no man is an island unto himself.

Nancy Leigh believes very strongly that we're supposed to be helping and encouraging each other so that those seeds of discouragement don't put down roots and turn to full-blown depression and anger and violence, as happens in so many lives, even in the church today.

In a presentation on encouragement, she urged us "to encourage one another daily, and these are some of the people who surround us in our daily lives. Ask the Lord to impress your heart: Who is someone that You've put in my life right now that You really want me to make an intentional effort to encourage?"

Still on people as source of encouragement, the church could be a veritable source of encouragement too. A brother told this story:

"I have not shied away from telling anyone who cares to listen how members of the local church I was introduced to when I arrived the United States, were useful to me and my family in our early days in this country.

It was not cathedral by size, but the relatively few worshipers of less than a hundred adults were there for me at every step. I joined the Pastor on a follow up visit after church service on a Sunday. He encouraged me with the assurance that two factors are mainly responsible for success of immigrants in this country: fear of God and hard work. He said he has seen the two factors in me and assured me that I will surely succeed in this my new-found home.

I vividly remember how a church brother paid my very first apartment rent. When word went around that I have gotten an apartment, from the very next day, church members donated all sort of household items to me so that I did not need to buy any item except for very personal items like bathing sponge, tooth brush and the likes.

With a shaky start up job, the church was always there to supplement my rent every month. When my family joined me, the entire women in the church rose in support, showering us with all sorts of gifts that overwhelmed us, and for which we are eternally grateful.

I make bold to state that the support I got from that parish, the Redeemed Christian Church of God, Mercy Seat Chapel in Gaithersburg, Maryland, gives me the meaning of the word encouragement and a practical example that the church exists to comfort and show care."

Through the church, some dear brothers and sisters in Christ, by their actions, words, notes, messages, and emails could be good sources of encouragement. When we do this, we are keeping to the instruction in Hebrews 10:25:

"And let us consider how to stir up one another to love and good works, not neglecting to meet together, as is the habit of some, but encouraging one another, and all the more as you see the day drawing near."

Now, the list of sources of encouragement cannot by any means be exhausted, but I must bring the individuals' own effort to stay encouraged to the fore and he or she can stay encouraged through the power of positive thinking.

Some call it faith-talk, others refer to it as self-motivation and belief system. Such internal speech to ourselves impacts our emotions, our behavior, our world view, and the manner we perceive and react to happenings around us.

How we respond to any situation is based on how we perceive the situation. Therefore, the Scripture says in Proverbs 23:7

"For as he thinks in his heart, so is he."

David Stoop explains, "It is not what is occurring in our lives that affects our behavior; it is what we believe about what is occurring that matters. If we focus on the facts related to an out-of-control world, we will behave in a certain manner. If we focus on a world under the control of an all-powerful God, we will behave in a different way."

Stoop goes ahead to give the illustration of the twelve men sent by Moses to spy out the land. These men all saw the same people and the same land but came back with two different reports. Ten of the spies were so scared of the Anaks, they developed a grasshopper mentality; their perspective was that Israel would be defeated. Only two believed that the Anaks could be defeated.

Joyce Meyer points out that, "The mind is the battlefield where we win or lose in life."

The mind is the reason why some people in the same profession are experts in what they do, while others struggle to barely make it.

Our mindset affects our how we see or know God. Very importantly, our mindset affects our faith level. Mindset makes some people to have great faith (Mathew 15), others have mustard seed faith (Mathew 17), while others suffer from terrible deficiency in faith.

Nothing enhances positive thinking like an absolute faith in God. Faith in God is not just a presumption, an impression, or an impulse. Rather it is the type of faith which Williams Ekanem describes this way in *Faith: The Believers' Rod:* It is a faith that: "gives the courage to face the present with confidence and future with expectancy."

To remain positive in our thinking is a function of our perception of God. Ekanem adds here that, "Faith is also how big or small your God is. Is He the omnipotent, omnipresent and omniscience God we read about to you? Or is He only the God of good times, and not of the tough times?"

Your answer to the above questions may give an indication as to how strong or weak your faith in God is. We must remember that in Daniel 3:18, the Hebrew boys did not demand that God prove Himself to them. They were willing to accept God's will, whatever it meant for them. They had faith and a positive thinking that was willing to accept whatever came their way as being part of God's plan for their lives and their faith, and guess what? They were richly rewarded.
Our thought system, at every point, should be inspired like that of the Apostle Paul. It was he who said, "Being fully persuaded that God had power to do what he had promised."

Such persuasion is a sure indication that God's promises in our lives will come to pass, regardless of how long it takes.

The last word in this chapter is that you act now by being a source of encouragement to someone. Take the advice of Doug Britton very seriously; don't start complaining as soon as you see your spouse, child, employee, neighbor, or anyone else.

Ask about his or her day. Give him or her a word of compliment. Share stories about your day, share insights from a Bible study, share victories on the job, or other things they may be interested in.

Acknowledge the abilities and efforts of the other person. If he or she feels inadequate, encourage him or her.

Monitor your positive and negative remarks. Learn to be self-aware and listen to what you say. Be sure you make many more positive comments than negative ones.

Respond to problems with encouragement. When someone talks about personal difficulties, do not respond with a "gloom and doom" attitude. Listen with compassion and avoid simplistic advice. Say something such as, "I know this is a tough time for you, but it won't last. Let me encourage you: God will see you through, and I'm here to help, too."

Understand that:

"God comforts us in all our troubles, so that we can comfort those in any trouble with the comfort we ourselves have received from God. 2 Corinthians 1:4

Remember and subscribe to apostle's advice to those in one situation or the other: *"And we urge you, brothers, warn those who are idle, encourage the timid, help the weak, be patient with everyone."* 1 Thessalonians 5:14

Discuss problems or issues as a friend and not as a foe. There are times in every relationship—in a family, on the job, or wherever—when people discuss difficult topics. When you do, please speak in a courteous, friendly manner. The way you speak usually is more important than whether your opinions are right or wrong.

As an exit line, let us not underestimate the power of a touch, a smile, a kind word, a listening ear, an honest compliment, or the smallest act of caring. All of these have the potential to encourage and turn a life around: do them now.

CHAPTER FIVE

Dangers of Discouragement

Discouragement is of the devil, and it is a very dangerous thing. It is apt to open this chapter with the popular story about a yard sale in Devil land. The devil was said to be putting up a yard sale of various items in his storehouse. The items were well laid out with prices marked on them for buyers. There were a lot of adverse emotional tools: hatred, envy, jealousy, deceit, pride, lying, and so on.

However, placed apart from the rest of the tools was a particular one. It was worn more than any of the others and was highly priced. "What's the name of this tool?" asked one of the potential customers. "That," the Devil replied, "is discouragement." Why have you priced it so high, the customer asked?

'Because discouragement is more useful to me than all the others. I can pry open and get inside a man's heart with it when I cannot get near him with any other tools. It's badly worn because I use it on almost everyone since so few people know it belongs to me."

The above story resonated very much with me because when people are discouraged, they refer to themselves as having a bad day. They do not know that it is a hidden tool of the devil to get the individual down. Discouragement is still the devil's tool today as it was in the days of old. Not many people realize the devil is using it on us even right now.

Life is not by any means a bed of roses; it is full of discouraging circumstances. Discouragement is a disease that is unique to human beings. It is a universal disease, and everyone gets it eventually. It does not exclude even the most blessed people, or the most successful, or the most spiritually mature; everyone face disappointment and discouragement. Discouragement affects seniors, adults, teenagers, and even infants. For all of us, there will be times when we want to give up, a time when we lose heart.

Not even men of God are spared from discouragement; in fact, they are about the most hit. Many renowned and successful pastors have struggled with discouragement. It is an ailment that afflicts Christians and keeps them from enjoying their relationship with God and with the brethren.

There is no doubt you've experienced discouragement at times, and maybe many times. You might even be discouraged at this very moment. It is good to know that you would honestly face problems (Job 14:1). Many people sugar-coat it and like referring to problems as challenges. When discouragement shows up, do not give up. Rather, acknowledge it and realize that you need help. Get the needed help, and most importantly, trust and obey God in the midst of the problems.

Why do we become discouraged? What are the causes of discouragement?

Built-up frustrations lead to discouragement. It happens most especially when an individual does the right things but experiences poor results. When an individual works very hard, for instance, and the pay is not commensurate with the job, the individual gets frustrated and ultimately discouragement sets in. The student who does all the homework and assignments, and studies hard but comes out with poor results gets discouraged. An individual who gets married, and several years after has no child, could face serious discouragement. A parent who trains a child, but the child grows into a nuisance, could also be discouraged. Discouragement is part of life, and we will discuss few of the causes:

Loss of Strength: *"Then Judah said, "The strength of the laborers is failing, and there is so much rubbish that we are not able to build the wall."* Nehemiah 4:10

This passage is a good example of loss of both physical and emotional strength. It could also be the loss of the willpower to continue.

As it happened in this story of rebuilding the wall, a combination of opposition and hard labor almost marred the vision of rebuilding the wall. The Scriptures added, however, 'But we built the wall, and the whole wall was joined to half its height, for the people had a mind to work." (Nehemiah 4:6)

We must give credit to the resolve, mindset, and focus of the people who persevered even in the face of mounting opposition:

"So it was, from that time on, that half of my servants worked at construction, while the other half held the spears, the shields, the bows, and wore armor; and the leaders were behind all the house of Judah." Nehemiah 4:16

And scorn:

'Now Tobiah the Ammonite was beside him, and he said, "Whatever

they build if even a fox goes up on it, he will break down their stone wall." Nehemiah 4:3.

In all these situations, the people were neither distracted nor intimidated. They had their eye on finishing the project, which they did, with God helping them. You will complete your project in Jesus name because the Scripture says, *"For if thou fail in the day of adversity, your strength is small."* Proverbs 24:10

Loss of strength could be caused by the fact that the newness of a project or a relationship has worn off. A time comes, the excitement about a particular thing diminishes. It is like a person who just bought a new car, and a time comes when the excitement and the smell of newness are gone. The owner then plans to trade it off.

At other times, it is the devil who wants to counter the vision. You start hearing comments like, "I think the Lord is leading us back," or "I don't think this is the plan of God."

Such words are the lie of the devil in the middle of a promising project that is only facing a natural down time. At such times, don't get tired. Be anxious for nothing. For we are not of them that draw back to perdition. Rather, renew your strength in the Lord, remind Him of His promise, and see the revival come through.

"But they that wait upon the Lord shall renew their strength; they shall mount up with wings as eagles; they shall run, and not be weary, and they shall walk, and not faint." Isaiah 40:31

It is time to reload and re-fire; it is not the time to give up!

Loss of Vision: Nehemiah 4:10

"...Yet there is much rubbish..."

"Yet" is an important word that communicates the thought of the people. Strength has begun to fail, despite the work which has been done. Many hang-ups, many carryover problems, many mistakes, many goof-ups, and many failures; yet, much rubbish.

Take for instance a young mother, changing five to ten diapers a day, and experiencing too much rubbish, too much mess. The baby has colic and will not stop crying. If she threw the child out the window on a 12-story building to his death, it will show that she has lost the vision. This is the same as some people at their jobs who start having some challenges, and the very next thing is to resign. Such resignation could be very premature because there are problems everywhere and one cannot continue running away. An individual who keeps throwing in the towel either has lost the vision or had no vision at the beginning. It must be said that when you don't have a vision, then you will start running other people's vision.

"And it shall come to pass afterward, that I will pour out my spirit upon all flesh; and your sons and your daughters shall prophesy, your old men shall dream dreams, your young men shall see visions," Joel 2:28.

Vision, even the one from God, does not take off like a rocket. Rather, God is a God of little beginnings (Zechariah 4:10). Jesus could have been born in the best inn in Bethlehem, but he was rather born in a manger. The vision may start slow, and as the Bible puts it, it may tarry; but it will see the light of the day if you persevere. Remember, the snail got inside the Ark of Noah.

Loss of Confidence: Nehemiah. 4:10

"...we ourselves are unable to rebuild the wall."

This comment is a devastating one. They started building the Wall; it was half way done. Why then can they not finish it? This scenario happens to virtually everyone. You start a project with an effusing confidence and high spirit, but something happened and all the zeal and confidence wane, discouragement sets in. When or if you find yourself in this state, consider the following:

a. *"The One Who called you is faithful and will do what He promised."* 1 Thessalonians 5:24.

b. When you lose strength, you lose vision and you lose confidence. Discouragement is at the door.

c. Like professional sport,– when you lose your vision, you will lose your confidence.

d. Note: They already built the wall halfway because "they had a mind to work" (Verse 6).

Fatigue: When you are physically or emotionally exhausted, you become a prime candidate to be infected with discouragement. Your defenses are lowered and things can seem more bleak than they really are.

When you are physically tired or you are experiencing fatigue, discouragement can quickly set in. For instance, when Elijah got the message from Jezebel in 1 Kings 19, discouragement set in; he became afraid and ran for his life into the wilderness. In that exhausted state, he prayed and said, "It's enough now, O Lord take my life.'

The Lord knew better and instead sent an angel to feed and comfort him:

"And the angel of the Lord came back the second time, and touched him, and said, Arise and eat, because the journey is too great for you." 1 Kings 19:7

Elijah was worn out, he was not thinking clearly, and he therefore became fearful. It is amazing to think that a man who shortly before supervised the execution of 450 prophets of Baal through the help of God, was now so scared of just a threat from Jezebel! When under excessive stress, your body will crave more rest and sleep than usual. Please, give in and rest.

Biologists confirm this because according to research, stress upsets your whole glandular system, it raises your blood pressure, and keeps body systems in a flight/fight state of tension. This constant state of ferment makes you vulnerable to everything from colds and muscular aches to ulcers, heart disease, and strokes. This reason is why ministers of God are often counseled to take proper rest, to eat well, and to exercise so they will be able to cope with the challenges of ministry.

Frustration: This is the precursor to discouragement. It is a state of disappointment that triggers discouragement and it is a state of reduced enthusiasm that happens when unfinished tasks pile up. It is a situation where we are not getting the result we expect. Frustration sets in when trivial matters or the unexpected interrupts you and prevents you from accomplishing what you really needed to do. Failed promises, failed expectations, unmet goals, tough times, impatience, and an inferiority complex can contribute to frustration. Frustration easily leads to discouragement.

But that should not be because, as Bernie Siege points out, that, "obstacles across our path can be spiritual flat tires---disruptions in our lives seem to be disastrous at the time, but end by redirecting our lives in a meaningful way."

Jesus must have known how easily some people will give up upon the slightest discouragement. He advised us in John 16: 33:

"In this world you will have trouble, but take heart! I have overcome the world."

Note that if you find a path with no obstacles, it is most likely a path that doesn't lead anywhere important. We should not take adversity as frustration, rather, it should spur us to look inwards and see the opportunity that God is bringing our way. Let us trust God enough to turn difficulty into opportunity. We can go from frustration to becoming focused and passionate. Remember, you must be a believer, if you would be an achiever.

King Solomon said in Ecclesiastes 9:10, "Whatever your hand finds to do, do it with all your might."

The moment you allow frustration to come in, your interest and your passion wanes. It is at these times that you need to remember that most winners are ex-losers. They are people who were once discouraged, but they became passionate and they overcame their frustration.

Failure: Sometimes, your best laid plans fall apart, the project collapses, the deal fails, and no one shows up to the event. How do you react? Do you give in to self-pity? Do you blame others? As one man said, "Just when I think I can make ends meet -- somebody moves the ends! That's discouraging!"

The fear of failure can be so devastating and it can discourage the victim from acting on their desires going forward. This fear of failure is particularly strong when the individual thinks of doing something he/she has never done before.

How we react to failure is what really matters because failure is often the first necessary step towards success. Life is a battle where we encounter a lot of failures. The widow that approached the unjust judge failed so many times to get justice (Luke 18:1-8), but that did not stop her from going back to the same judge until she got what she wanted.

The single most important difference between champions and average people is their ability to handle rejection and failure.

If we don't risk failing, we don't get the chance to succeed. Against all odds and polls, Donald Trump won the 2016 United States presidential election even with a more visible, experienced opponent. He was never deterred, even with glaring prospects of failure. No one sets out to fail, but let your failure rather than discourage you, be the stepping stone to propel you to victory. Let your days of failure be the best time to sow your seeds of success. Learn how to fail intelligently and when you fall, pick something up, go from failure, and learn something new!

Fear: Fear is behind more discouragement than we would like to admit. The fear of criticism: "What will they think?" The fear of responsibility: "What if I can't handle this?" The fear of failure: "What if I blow it?" The fear of not pleasing God, fear of making a mistake, fear of change, or fear of sacrifice, can cause a major upset in the life of an individual. Fear is said to be faith in reverse. Fear wants you to run even from things and people that are not after you. Job was a man of fear: first, he feared for his children and their daily activities; he would sanctify them after every feast and offer burnt offerings on their behalf lest they have sinned in their hearts. When he eventually experienced bouts of troubles he said, 'For the thing I greatly feared has come upon me, and what I dreaded has happened to me." Job 3:25.

John Mason shares that fear is a poor chisel to carve out your tomorrow. You will get defeated by your fear even before you venture out to do anything of substance.

Joyce Meyer notes that, 'Whether its low-level nervousness or full blown panic, most of us experience some degree of fear when we think of doing something new. Our minds are filled with excitement, yet we think, what if this? What if that? What if ? What if ?"

Bible scholars say "fear not" is mentioned 367 times in the Bible, approximately one for each day of the year, thus teaching us how to handle fear.

A great word of encouragement against fear is seen in Isaiah 41:10:

'Fear not, for I am with you; Be not dismayed, for I am your God. I will strengthen you, Yes, I will help you, I will uphold you with My righteous right hand."

We must know that every new level has a new devil to deal with. We must know that we must go through the pain to get to the gain.

Ironically, the Bible is replete with those who experienced

moments of discouragement. It is interesting that they all overcame it and went ahead to do great exploits.

Paul's treacherous companions

Those Christians who are expressing frustrations with the hardships that they are experiencing even though they are workers in the vineyard should borrow a leaf from the Apostle Paul. Paul suffered persecution from those who were co-workers and had all the reasons to be discouraged, but he lived above it.

A good recap of some of the things Paul suffered is in 2 Corinthians 11:16-33, where he personally recounted what he went through: worked harder, imprisoned, flogged severally, shipwrecked, endangered, sleepless, hungry, thirsty; but instead of wallowing in self-pity and discouragement, Paul instead boasted about his sufferings for Christ.

He instead used one of his epistle to encourage Timothy and by extension Christians to persevere in the cause of Jesus Christ and to endure hardship. He wrote this while he was in prison and he was close to his death.

Paul warned of hard times ahead. He warned of increasing persecution and proliferation of false teachers who will infiltrate the church, just as is happening today. Paul called out some people that he was particularly disappointed with; people such as Hymenaeus, Demas, and Alexander the coppersmith. It is on record that Alexander incited the people against Paul and caused an uproar in Ephesus (Acts 19: 21-41).

In his charge to Timothy, shortly before his death, he reflected on the activities of Alexander and said, "Alexander the coppersmith did me much harm. May the Lord repay him according to his works." 2 Timothy 4:14.

Ain Wang writes about Alexander this way: Paul complained bitterly about a lot of people and what they did to him. One of those people was Alexander the Coppersmith. This man must have hurt Paul so badly that he had previously warned Timothy in his first letter 1 Timothy 1:20.

The coppersmith felt threatened with Paul's preaching. Many of the adherents of Artemis deserted the idol and with that Alexander's hope of their purchasing the statue of the goddess. Alexander initiated a riot and chaos in the city and made it difficult for Paul to preach the gospel of Christ in Ephesus.

We have many Alexander the coppersmiths in our lives, in our places of work, family, business, career, and even in ministry. They will do everything to contradict the good that we stand for. They are contrary to us, just to keep their territories protected. It would not matter to them whether their contradictory acts will be for the common good or not. Their one concern is their selfish end. They will not only contradict the good that we try to do, they will also struggle to get other good people on their side. They create camps, so that we may not succeed in doing good. Many of them are like the dog in the manger. They will not use the place for themselves and they will prevent anyone from using the place.

You share your secret with them, but they go behind your back and divulge it to others. They make life difficult for you, they make it difficult for you to trust anyone. There could be great danger and indeed discouragement from such false brethren; they are worse than open enemies.

It is dangerous to have anything to do with those who would be enemies to such a man as Paul. But if we hand them over to God, the Lord will stand by us, and strengthen us in our difficulties and dangers. His presence will more than supply every one of our needs.

Elijah's crushing discouragement

"And Ahab told Jezebel all that Elijah had done, also how he had executed all the prophets with the sword. 2 Then Jezebel sent a messenger to Elijah, saying, "So let the gods do to me, and more also, if I do not make your life as the life of one of them by tomorrow about this time." 3 And when he saw that, he arose and ran for his life, and went to Beersheba, which belongs to Judah, and left his servant there." 1 Kings 19:1-3

The Prophet Elijah moved from a soaring victory to a crushing discouragement as represented in the verses above. Remember that we stated at the beginning of this chapter that discouragement sets in when an individual does the right things but experiences poor results. After one of the greatest triumphs in the history of Israel, and the annihilation of 450 prophets of Baal, Elijah expected that a great spiritual revival and accompanying positive turnaround of the people would happen. Not only did it not happen, but the next thing that happened to him was to be threatened and taunted by Jezebel. He was greatly disillusioned.

His absurd reaction makes his action a continual reference point in biblical discussion of discouragement. Elijah reacted by running away. Out of fear, he ran as much as 80 miles to the wilderness of Beersheba. He forgot, entirely, all his victories.

Often, when things do not go the way we anticipated, we also get disappointed. Some of us will even grumble; we also forget all we have accomplished before the trial of faith.

In his discouraged state, Elijah exaggerated his problem like some people do today. He looked down on himself as not better than his fathers and he stated that he preferred to die.

Gavin Ortlund describes it this way:

"This is not a fear of dying, but the kind of fear that makes you want to die. This is the fear of deep discouragement, the fear of a crushed spirit, which enshrouds you in the lonely moments of life."

No one has ever successfully run away from problems. Before long, God caught up with him and asked him a pointed question:

"*...what are you doing here, Elijah?*" I Kings 19: 9.

Elijah's predicament reminds one of the story of Jonah, who also wanted to run away from God. It also reminds us about what David stated in Psalms 139:7-12 when he asked: "where can I go from your spirit?"

His response that he has been zealous for God, yet they want to kill him, gives credence to our premise that Elijah was primarily discouraged because of his failed expectation regarding the outcome of his triumphs and the subsequent threat from Jezebel.

God in His infinite mercies was very patient with Elijah by sending an angel to feed and comfort him. God also occupied him with other responsibilities. (1 Kings 19:15-18)

We must note that Elijah, like most Ministers of God today, measured ministry by his own expectations rather than by the purpose of God. We must learn that indeed, it is not by might, but by the spirit. We must realize that God does not reward success, but obedience. God holds us responsible for trusting in Him, for obedience, for love, for endurance, and for faithfulness to do what He has called us to do. It is He who gives the increase or success.

We cannot complete this portrait of discouraged prophets of the Bible without reflecting on **Moses' discouraging moments.**

Moses diligently obeyed and did what God sent him, yet the result was not what he expected. The task masters increased the burden of the Israelites and the people blamed Moses for their problems. Moses did not bargain for this response. He had thought God would deliver the people immediately, even though God had told him He would harden Pharaoh's heart (Exodus 5).

In Numbers 11, when the people started complaining about all they are missing because they left Egypt, Moses said

"So the children of Israel also wept again and said, who will give us meat to eat? We remember the fish which we ate freely in Egypt, the cucumbers, the melons, the leeks, the onions, and the garlic; but now our whole being is dried up, there is nothing at all except this manna before our eyes." Numbers 11: 4-6.

This act of ingratitude greatly displeased Moses, who believed that God has done them a lot of good by taking them out of the land of suffering. Moses' displeasure must have increased in intensity more so as the people were not only complaining, but they were weeping aloud and expressing their disappointment with Moses for exposing them to hardship.

The Bible records that 'Moses was displeased;" one can also say discouraged:

"So Moses said to the Lord, why have You afflicted Your servant? And why have I not found favor in Your sight, that You have laid the burden of all these people on me? Did I conceive all these people? Did I beget them, that You should say to me, carry them in your bosom, as a guardian carries a nursing child, to the land which You swore to their fathers."

This was the height of Moses' discouragement with the task of leading the people out of suffering to a land flowing with milk and honey. As divine as the task undertaken by Moses was, he was still exposed to moments of discouragement. This mindset eventually pushed him to strike the rock instead of speaking to the rock for water as instructed by God. As it is with those in ministry, discouragement left unchecked might lead to a more dangerous outcome like Moses being disallowed to enter Canaan.

C.S. Lewis wrote that if the devil's arsenal of weapons were restricted to a single piece of equipment, it would be discouragement. Charles Spurgeon sums it up this way:

"Elijah, due to discouragement, failed in the very point at which he was strongest. Most men fail where they feel really strong. In scripture, it is the wisest man who proves himself to be the greatest fool; just as the meekest man, Moses, spoke hasty and bitter words. Abraham failed in his faith, and Job in his patience; so, Elijah who was the most courageous of all men, fled from an angry woman."

The discouragement at Gethsemane:

Not even Jesus Christ, the savior of the world, was spared of discouraging moments while on earth. But for His focus, passion, and comfort by angel, the discouraging moments when Christ felt the pains of his punishment by the people of the world could have overwhelmed him.

According to the synoptic gospels, immediately after the Last Supper, Jesus moved away to pray. Each Gospel offers a slightly different account regarding the narrative.

Matthew and Mark identify this place of prayer as Gethsemane. Jesus was accompanied by the Apostles Peter, John, and James, whom he asked to stay awake and pray. He moved "a stone-throw away" from them. In this place, He felt overwhelming sadness and anguish, and he said:

"My Father, if it is possible, let this cup pass me by. Nevertheless, let it be as you, not I, would have it." Then, a little while later, He said, "If this cup cannot pass by, but I must drink it, your will be done!" Matthew 26:42.

He said this prayer three times, checking on the three apostles between each prayer and finding them asleep. He commented: "The spirit is willing, but the flesh is weak." An angel came from heaven to strengthen him during his agony and as he prayed,

"His sweat was as it were great drops of blood falling down upon the ground." Luke 22:44.

The events that occurred in the Garden of Gethsemane

have reverberated down through the centuries. The passion Jesus displayed on that momentous night has been depicted in music, books, and films for centuries. From the 16th century, when Bach wrote two magnificent oratorios based on the gospel accounts of Matthew and John, to the present day with the film *The Passion of the Christ*, the story of this extraordinary night has been told again and again. Even our language has been affected by these events, giving us such phrases as *"he who lives by the sword dies by the sword"* Matthew 26:52; *"the spirit is willing, but the flesh is weak"* Mark 14:38; and *"sweating drops of blood"* Luke 22:44.

Of course, the most important impact of this night was the willingness of our Savior to die on the cross in our place to pay the penalty for our sins. God "made Him who knew no sin, to be sin for us, that we might become the righteousness of God in Him" 2 Corinthians 5:21.

Eli, Eli, Lama Sabachthani

One of the greatest triggers of discouragement is to feel forsaken. At the moment Jesus Christ made the famous comments, he was a candidate for discouragement:

"And about the ninth hour Jesus cried with a loud voice, saying, Eli, Eli, lama sabachthani? that is to say, My God, my God, why hast thou forsaken me?" Mathew 27:46

This was a critical moment for Jesus; it was the darkest three hours in the history of mankind. Mathew Henry Commentary says

"Jesus was in agony, wrestling with the powers of darkness, and suffering his Father's displeasure against the sin of man, for which he was now making his soul an offering. Never were there three such hours since the day God created man upon the earth, never such a dark and awful scene."

Jesus underwent great bodily sufferings; he was flogged and the enemies reviled him. Anybody would be discouraged, but not Jesus. After the statement, His accusers said He was calling on Elijah to help him, but rather than showing compassion by offering any help, they instead taunted Him the more and showed how wicked humans can be:

"Immediately one of them ran and took a sponge, filled it with sour wine and put it on a reed, and offered it to Him to drink. The rest said, 'let Him alone; let us see if Elijah will come to save Him.'" Matthew 27:47 - 49

Just before he finally gave up the ghost, Jesus spoke again. He decided to show that his life was not forcefully taken away from him, but that he freely delivered it into his Father's hands because He had undertaken to make himself an offering for sin. Jesus willingly gave up his life.

CHAPTER SIX

Encouragement and the End Game

"I have fought the good fight, I have finished the race, I have kept the faith." 2 Timothy 4:7

Besides biblical stories, not many come back experiences are as encouraging as that of Bessie Coleman, as told by Joyce Meyer. Bessie Coleman was a beautiful, vivacious, and courageous young woman who came to be known as *Queen Bess*. She was the first African-American licensed pilot and the first American woman to earn an international pilot's license. Before she accomplished these remarkable achievements, Coleman dreamed of adventures in her hometown of Atlanta, Texas. When she was twenty-three years old, she finally ventured outside the confines of small-town life and moved to the big city of Chicago to be near several of her other 12 biological brothers and sisters and to pursue a life that had been beyond her reach in Atlanta, Texas.

In Chicago, Bessie worked as a manicurist in a barber shop, where she listened to stories about World War 1 pilots and their adventures in the sky. She dreamed of becoming a pilot herself, but could not afford to do so. At the barbershop, Coleman met two influential businessmen who helped fund her training. One was a newspaper man who thought her story would be good for business. Because flight schools in America did not train black women, Bessie studied diligently to learn French and moved to Paris to attend flight school in 1920.

Upon her return to America, she gained much media attention, and people of all races embraced her as they learned about her in the newspapers. Throughout her career, she participated in air shows and was invited to attend important events.

Bessie Coleman died in a plane crash, probably resulting from a wrench in one of the gears, on April 30, 1926, and more than ten thousand people attended the funeral of this courageous young woman who refused to give up.

Meyer summarized the story this way:

"Bessie Coleman faced much discouragement and many obstacles because American flight schools refused to accept her and she had to put her dreams on hold while making an effort involved in learning a foreign language. She had to move alone to a new country, which took great boldness for the determined young woman. Even though her path to success was not as easy as those of her white counterparts, she found a way to do what she wanted. It required extra time and effort, but she did not let fear or the uncertainties of moving to a foreign country keep her from pursuing her dream---because she was determined not to give up."

In discussing the end game of encouragement, it makes sense to consider those factors that aided the turnaround, the metamorphosis from despair to hope, from failure to accomplishment and self-actualization.

A top factor that facilitates turnaround from discouragement is a *total dependence* on God. We must not depend on our contacts or our credentials because the arm of flesh does fail. This assertion brings to fore, John 15:5, where Christ says, "I am the vine; you are the branches. If you remain in me and I in you, you will bear much fruit; apart from me you can do nothing."

Most times, regardless of the inconvenience we are going through, we hold out, thinking that we can handle it on our own, but we eventually failed and got discouraged. The Israelites, during their sojourn, started on this wrong route and would undergo self-inflicted suffering for years before it dawned on them to call on God Almighty for help.

Judges 6: 1-6 is just one example, and verse 6 specifically says:

'So Israel was greatly impoverished because of the Midianites, and the children of Israel cried out to the Lord."

Reading further down, we see that God indeed answered their cries and sent a deliverer. However, why did they wait so long to turn to the Lord? The answer to this question is still relevant today, as it was in their situation, because they waited until every seemingly possible option played out. These days, calling on 911, relying on insurance and medical doctors, relying on one's fat bank account and the like, is often the first recourse before many of us remember to take the situation to God in prayer.

As rich, well-connected and educated as we may be, we must know that, "Unless the Lord builds the house, the builders labor in vain. Unless the Lord watches over the city, the guards stand watch in vain," Psalm 127:1.

We must depend upon God's blessings and not our contrivances. Everything that we have comes from God. He is the one who gives us the power to make wealth. In 1 Corinthians 4:7 the Apostle Paul asked the question:

"What do you have that you did not receive?"

If we believe that everything that we possess comes from God, we must depend on Him as our great provider and our deliverer.

Testimonies abound where those who depend entirely on God eventually have a personal encounter with His presence. This personal encounter with His presence is the second factor that aids turnaround from discouragement. All those who ended well in the Bible had a personal encounter with God. Every discouraged person needs a personal encounter with God to get out of that state.

Peter gave us an experiential knowledge of the goodness of God's presence during a discouraging fishing expedition. Jesus stepped into his boat after a night long of fruitless labor. When God shows up, there is liberty, deliverance, comfort, and promotion. The Lord God Almighty will show up for you in Jesus name.

Very close to personal encounter is the hand of God. The concept of the hand of God is an anthropomorphic term. This term is used to attribute certain human physical characteristics to God. It is an attempt to give us a better understanding of God who is a spirit (John 4:24).

God's hand can turn around discouragement. God's hands are His power, strength, and His ability. Isaiah 66:2 says His hands make everything and Acts 7:50 corroborates it with:

"Was it not my hand that made all these things?"

The mighty hand of God will deliver you from discouragement and the enemy. He will set you free and take you out of the pit of sorrows. He will destroy the trigger that prompts discouragement. God's promises about His hands and us are as found in Isaiah 41:10, Psalm 110:1, and Exodus 6:1. It is unequivocal that we are serving a God of all comfort. He is the father of compassion who comforts us in all our troubles (2 Corinthians 1:3-4), even in discouraging times. He is a great provider. Our God is the God of providence. He actively rules over the world, and He controls the affairs of men. The knowledge of His rule should give us the confidence that He can turn around our discouraging situations.

Other factors such as how we respond to the discouraging situations, being forward looking and not looking back, could also influence how an individual finishes his or her race.

It is often said that many were called, but few are chosen. Unfortunately, many characters in the Bible did not finish strong; they ended so disappointingly for various reasons. Although some of them started very well, their ending is not worth emulating. Take Solomon, for instance, the cherished son of the mighty king David who built the temple of God. 1 Kings 11:9-10 states that, "The Lord became angry with Solomon because his heart had turned away from the Lord… although He had forbidden Solomon to follow other gods, Solomon did not keep the Lord's command."

Others in this basket of failures include Saul, Hezekiah, Asa, Uzziah, Josiah, Judas, Demas, Gideon, and many others.

Conversely, there are those worthy of emulation; they finished well. By their determination to finish strong, they have become role models to genuine Christians today.

Take the Apostle Paul as an example. Bob Stone, at a pastor's seminar, said, "The apostle was obsessed with finishing well."

According to Stone, Paul saw life as a race and was so motivated to finish well that he challenged the Corinthian believers to run the race in such a way as to get the prize... and...not run aimlessly(1 Corinthians 9: 24-26). In that passage, Paul described his disciplined training, saying that he disciplined his body to make it do what it must, not what it wanted, so that, 'having preached to others, I myself will not be disqualified for the prize."

Besides the Corinthians, Paul also addressed the Ephesians on the import of finishing well. When meeting with the Ephesian elders for the last time, he told them, "I consider my life worth nothing to me, if only I may finish the race and complete the task the Lord has given me...the task of testifying to the good news of God's grace." Acts 20:24

In a very emotion-laden letter to his disciple, Timothy, in 2 Timothy 4: 6-8, Paul looks forward upon his death with the assurance that, "He has fought the good fight and finished the race."

He was not afraid of death because he had the testimony of his conscience, which by the grace of God, he had in some good measure answered the ends of living.

Paul's strong finishing becomes even more resonating when considered against all that he went through, as he recounted in 2 Corinthians 11:16-33, where he boasted about his sufferings instead of grumbling, as many of us would have done or are doing today.

Paul took whatever came his way as momentary, always looking forward to an eternal glory as he encouraged the church at Corinth in 2 Corinthians 4:16-17:

"Therefore we do not lose heart. Even though our outward man is perishing, yet the inward man is being renewed day by day. 17 For our light affliction, which is but for a moment, is working for us a far more exceeding and eternal weight of glory."

This mindset shows that how an individual responds to a situation and a forward-looking perspective could be very useful factors in finishing strong.

Joseph was another individual who finished strong in the

Bible. Not so many people in the Bible went through what Joseph suffered. Almost at every turn, and wherever he found himself, he faced deep suffering and yet, he finished strong.

Joseph's experience was made worse by the fact that his travails originated from within, from his brothers, his flesh and blood, who started it all when they sold him out with the apparent intention to eliminate him from the family inheritance. But because God was with him, it turned out good for him, as we read in Genesis 50: 20:

"You intended to harm me, but God intended it good to me."

Joseph had an opportunity at pay back when the brothers, stricken by hunger in the land, went looking for food. He was in authority, and he had the capacity to do them harm. As a God- fearing person, however, he left vengeance unto God. During the ugly episode with Potiphar's wife, a weak-minded person would have fallen for seduction, but Joseph's high moral standard and more importantly, Joseph's fear of God, influenced his choice in life.

For an individual who languished in jail for a better part of two years because of offense he didn't commit, that experience would have become a source of great bitterness for many modern Christians, but Joseph persevered. The fact that his passionate request to the butler to mention him to the king was not carried out would have discouraged many people, and they would have questioned God, but not Joseph.

We can say that the bitter experiences Joseph went through were enough to discourage anybody and should have made him throw in the towel. Not Joseph! He overcame personal failures and major setbacks by embracing the grace of God. Joseph finished strong and even prophesied shortly before he passedon. In the account of those who finished strong in the Bible, it is noteworthy to highlight how an uncompromising faithled Daniel to finish strong.

The entire story of Daniel and how he finished well can be summarized into three categories:

Category 1: He started right

Category 2: He maintained the initial commitment without wavering

Category 3: He ultimately finished strong

Daniel's faith and unfettered devotion to God was exemplary. He started right by refusing to defile himself with King Nebuchadnezzar's food and wine but instead requested only vegetables and water (Daniel1:16-18).

To show that this commitment was not a fluke, he maintained his faith in God by praying three times a day to God almighty even when a decree was issued that no one should pray to any god or man except to the king for thirty days. When he faced punishment for undertaking these prayers, and he was about to be thrown into Lion's Den, Daniel's faith was unwavering, and he was not afraid; instead, he was completely devoted to God almighty.

One underlying factor that sees many cross the finish line is utmost faith in God. This was greatly demonstrated in the life of Abraham, the father of faith. Derek Hill, in his series on ten inspirational Bible characters, describes Abraham as, "a real man of faith."

In the amazing faith story of Abraham, Abraham and Sarah were without children at old age. Abraham was a hundred years old, and Sarah was ninety when God promised them a son. This did not happen immediately; the child came only after several years of frustration. Abraham spoke about this frustration in Genesis 15:2-3.

"But Abram said, "Lord God, what will You give me, seeing I go childless, and the heir of my house is Eliezer of Damascus?" 3 Then Abram said, "Look, You have given me no offspring; indeed one born in my house is my heir!"

Abraham felt that it was over with him taking into consideration his age. When the promise came, however, it rekindled his faith. The word of God will rekindle your faith in Jesus name.

The eventual birth of Isaac, the promised child, was such a great joy to Abraham and Sarah, so much that Sarah made the now famous statement in Genesis 21: 6-7:

"And Sarah said, God has made me laugh, and all who hear will laugh with me." 7 She also said, "Who would have said to Abraham that Sarah would nurse children? For I have borne him a son in his old age."

Ordinarily, besides the grief of sending away Hagar the maid servant and her son Ishmael, one would say things were going very fine with Abraham and the wife, but then, it happened, Abraham's faith in God was tested when God said to Abraham:

"Take now thy son, thine only son Isaac, whom thou lovest, and get thee into the land of Moriah and offer him there for a burnt-offering upon one of the mountains which I will tell thee of." Genesis 22:2

Now, God was very specific in this instruction to Abraham; he mentioned the name, Isaac. Knowing the inherently crafty nature of man, God did not want Abraham to second guess which of the sons, and maybe attempt to go for Ishmael, which would have seemed reasonable, considering that this was a child born out of wedlock. Because He knows our thoughts, God knew how Abraham loved his promised son Isaac, so God qualified His request with "whom thou lovest," to avoid any misunderstanding or misrepresentation as to whom He wanted for the sacrifice.

Going by this account, it must have, without a doubt, been a very difficult time for Abraham. He was faced with the choice of either obeying divine instruction or keeping his child. This is a situation that constantly replays itself today in the lives of many Christians. God wanted to see if Abraham loved Him more than Isaac. We have today, very similar situations. Couples experience barrenness, go into intense prayers and fasting; God answers with gift of a child or children and that child or children become the sole reason the couple is increasingly getting cold in the house of God. They are no longer on fire for God, they dump their first love, with excuses that always revolve around the children.

But Abraham passed the test; you will pass your test in Jesus name, he obeyed. Abraham's obedience is unique. It was not a day's journey to the spot of sacrifice; the scripture records in Genesis 22:4 that, "then on the third day, Abraham lifted up his eyes, and saw the place far off."

This was not a few hours or one-day journey, but a three-day journey. Abraham had more than enough time to change his mind. Many Christians today would rationalize the instruction from God and say Satan get thee behind me. In these days of Christianity of convenience, where church members espouse liberty, freedom in Christ, and leaders are more bent in getting honorariums than sacrificial service, many would have failed this test, but Abraham obeyed.

God was indeed so moved by this great show of obedience that He made a declaration:

"By Myself I have sworn, says the Lord, because you have done this thing, and have not withheld your son, your only son— 17 blessing I will bless you, and multiplying I will multiply your descendants as the stars of the heaven and as the sand which is on the seashore, and your descendants shall possess the gate of their enemies. 18 In your seed, all the nations of the earth shall be blessed because you have obeyed My voice." Genesis 22: 16-18

This was the defining moment for Abraham, and he did not crash it. With this, previous mistakes of Abraham like denying his wife before Abimelech, became a non-issue. Abraham had proven his love for God Almighty and he indeed finished strong. The list of those that ended well in the Bible despite very challenging situations is numerous, and we cannot go into each situation, think of Noah, the man of endurance; David, the man after God's heart; Job, the one who persevered; Mary, who loved the Lord, and a host of others.

We must make a final mention concerning the author and finisher of our faith, the sacrificial lamb, Jesus Christ. He "came to His own, and His own did not receive Him." (John 1:11)

Jesus came as the Messiah to Israel, the King of the Kingdom of Heaven, but Israel rejected Him. In the few years that He ministered on earth, He showed forth God as the Father. Jesus was the only one who combined divinity and humanity that is being fully human-divine and fully human (John 1:1). With this combination, it means Jesus tasted suffering even on a scale much greater than that of any other human being, he suffered temptations like every other man and most importantly suffered death for sins He did not commit sin as explained in Hebrews 4:15:

"For we do not have a High Priest who cannot sympathize with our weaknesses, but was in all points tempted as we are, yet without sin."

During His time on earth, He preached life-changing sermons and taught intriguing parables that continue to challenge today's most intellectual minds. He healed hundreds of incurable diseases, fed thousands miraculously, calmed storms instantly, walked on water unflinchingly, raised people from the dead, handpicked and trained just a dozen men, eleven of whom would go on to change the world forever by spreading the Good News of Christ.

An indisputable truth that Jesus finished strong can be seen from the account in Mark 16: 19:

"So then, after the Lord had spoken to them, He was received up into heaven, and sat down at the right hand of God."

He was glorified in heaven with the glory He had while on earth. The question now is what can we learn from those that finished strong? Joseph Stanko, president of Purpose Quest International, gave the answer in the following guidelines during one of his seminars:

1. **Maintain holy living.** There is no greater obstacle to finishing well than sin. Sin tarnishes the best of records and intentions. You must always allow the Holy Spirit to work with you to ensure that you become more like Jesus.

This involves a commitment to prayer, fellowship and Bible study. And don't ignore issues such as anger, which caused Moses to miss entering the promised land. Make every effort to live a holy and obedient life.

2. **Know your purpose.** Paul could say that he had finished the race because he knew what his race entailed. Jesus finished the work the Father gave Him to do. Both knew their reasons for being here and stayed true to their work. In re-examining the list, it is obvious that the most successful finishers knew their purpose and stayed true to it to the end.

3. **Be true to your purpose.** Both Solomon and King Saul knew their purposes, but they got sidetracked by selfish ambition and personal pleasure. The Pharisees rejected God's purpose, and that marked the beginning of the end for their movement and way of life, Luke 7:30. The best finishers, such as Jesus, Paul, and Joseph, were productive to the end.

4. **Leave some legacy.** You don't have to construct a building or start a movement named after you to leave a spiritual legacy. Of the characters we studied, some wrote, others had family who carried on their name or work, still others left a body of work that could be emulated.

Finishing well requires that you think through what you will leave behind that has the potential to bless others after you're gone. There is no guarantee that will happen, for only God can provide that kind of impact. But those who finish well think about what they have the power to produce that can pass on to people the work God has done in their lives.

5. **Leave behind a good name.** Proverbs 10:7 says, "the memory of the righteous is blessed, but the name of the wicked will rot." That's quite a statement!

What kind of name does King Saul have among Bible readers? What about Solomon? Paul? Samson? The Pharisees?

Not many people are remembered beyond one or two generations after their deaths. So if nothing else, you can finish well by leaving behind a good name that your children and grandchildren can remember.

Ultimately, it is most important to finish strong in God's eyes. When Martin Luther King Jr. was assassinated, not many people were happy with the job he was doing. Today there aren't too many cities in the United States that don't have some memorial to his work and name.

CHAPTER SEVEN

The Cultural Dimension of Encouragement

"Therefore, brethren, stand fast and hold the traditions which you were taught, whether by word or our epistle." 2 Thessalonians 2:15

Encouragement, both at the individual and corporate level, is a great form of relationship building. Christianity in all its intents and purposes is about creating a better relationship between God and man.

It would amount to a futile exercise to attempt to "go and make disciples," which is the great commission if one cannot develop and build a good relationship between oneself and the potential disciples.

The gospel points out in Mathew 25:41-46, the danger of not helping or rendering support to the needy.

The urgent and great need for encouragement amongst Christians was again demonstrated in James 2:15 and 16, where the scriptures specifically used this example to bring home its message:

"If a brother or sister is naked and destitute of daily food, and one of you says to them, "Depart in peace, be warmed and filled," but you do not give them the things which are needed for the body, what does it profit?"

The primary duty of a believer is akin to the core principles of Public Relations. A communication marketing strategy is to build and create a mutual relationship between individuals and or organizations. This is also the core responsibility of a Christian. We must do good as instructed in Philippians 4:8:

"Finally, brethren, whatever things are true, whatever things are noble, whatever things are just, whatever things are pure, whatever things are lovely, whatever things are of good report, if there is any virtue and if there is anything praiseworthy—meditate on these things."

Just as in Public Relations, culture is yet to be effectively integrated into evangelism. This cultural integration is a reason some Bible Colleges are progressively introducing cross-cultural communication into their curriculum. Krishnamurthy Sriramesh, a communications specialist, points out that much of culture related literature and scholarship in this area continue to be ethnocentric with a predominantly American and to lesser extent British and Western European bias. This bias is to the detriment of other parts of the world.

However, in a rapidly globalizing world, evangelists will ignore the influence of culture to their peril if they are to effectively carry out the great commission.

We must ask ourselves this question: what is culture? In its simplest terms, culture is a way of life of a people; it is the set of predominating attitudes and behavior that characterize a group, which could be an organization, class, community or nation. When these attitudes or modes get passed down from one generation to another, it becomes a tradition.

Without boring us with the semantics, we would be using the words culture and tradition interchangeably. It is wonderful to realize that even the Bible recognizes the existence of our customs and traditions. In 2 Thessalonians 2:15, the Apostle Paul enjoined them to, "Therefore, brethren, stand fast and hold the traditions which you were taught, whether by word or our epistle."

The food a community eats, the language they speak, race, hobbies, religion, socioeconomic status, worldview, etc., combine to make up the culture of a group of people or nation. It is important to note that there are indeed other variables or local variations of the above factors that also need to be identified and integrated. In other words, culture or traditions are not homogeneous but rather heterogeneous depending on the history of the group under study.

For instance, the Excellence Project, a study in communications management, identifies other variables such as the political system, media system, economic system, and level of activism as other factors that affect the cultural identity of a group.

We can assess the effect of culture on encouragement, in other words, we can evaluate how people are influenced in their attitude to encouragement by the dictates of their societal culture. How does an individual's cultural background affect his/her level of encouragement?

Without going into detailed analysis of empirical data, we will provide a little synopsis of the cultural value in all the continents to give a clue to the prevalent culture of encouragement in these places.

The parameters in gauging the level of encouragement in a particular society would be taken from the religion, customs, family structure, and etiquette of the people.

Australia: Australians have a *"mateship,"* culture which is anti-hierarchical. Here, everyone is expected to behave with humility and not think of themselves as better than their peers. In this culture, any disloyalty to their *"mates"* is treated harshly and highly criticized. In this culture, even the most successful are eager to proclaim how ordinary they are, to the extent that two-thirds of the highest earning households define themselves as middle class.

Australia has no state religion, although with 61 percent are Christians, it has a strong tradition of secular government, religious organizations have played a significant role in public life. The Christian churches, in particular, have played an integral role in the development of education, health, and welfare services. While less than a quarter of Christians attend church weekly, around a quarter of all school students attend church-affiliated schools and the Christian festivals of Easter and Christmas are public holidays. The Roman Catholic Church is by far the largest non-government provider of health and education services in Australia.

In greetings, most forms of address are by first name or nickname, and only children regularly use titles such as "Sir" or "Ma'am" for authority figures.

The *mateship* culture combined with the original convict and then colonial culture has created an irreverence for established authority, particularly if it is pompous or out of touch with reality. Rather there is the popular Aussie modesty culture and Australians are very down to earth and always mindful of not giving the impression that they think they are better than anyone else. They value authenticity, sincerity, and loathe pretentiousness, and prefer people who are modest, humble, self- deprecating, and with a sense of humor.

Australians do not draw attention to their academic or other achievements and tend to distrust people who do.

They often downplay their own success, which may make them appear not to be achievement-oriented.

Australians place a high value on relationships; with a relatively small population, it is important to get along with everyone, since you never know when your paths may cross again. This leads to a win-win negotiating style since having everyone come away with positive feelings helps facilitate future business dealings, the spirit of encouragement thrives, and individuals do everything to give a helping hand to the other prison.

The import of a culture where no one thinks of himself as superior to the other but sees everyone as equal is likely to be heavy in giving help and support to the less fortunate or down trodden, more so when the people are predominantly Christians. The Apostle John writes

"If anyone has material possessions and sees his brother in need but has no pity on him, how can the love of God be in him?" 1 John 3:17-18.

When this passage is combined with what the gospel enjoins us on equality (James 2:1-4), then it could be said that there is a great deal of encouragement amongst people from Australia.

Europe: It is impossible to form a single, all-embracing conception of European culture, rather the culture here might better be described as a series of overlapping cultures. Whether it be a question of West as opposed to East; Catholicism and Protestantism as opposed to Eastern Orthodoxy; Christianity as opposed to Islam; many have claimed to identify cultural fault lines across the continent.

That notwithstanding, it can be said that the influence of Christianity on Europe is huge. Christianity has remained Europe's main religion though it was broken into different branches: Orthodox, Protestant, and Catholic, and depending on the beliefs of different regions, people adopted them. Judaism is also practiced in Europe, and the religion of Sunni' Islam is practiced in Turkey and some southern parts of Europe.

The World Region Project states that in lifestyle, Europe is divided into four traditional cultural areas: The Atlantic Fringe, The Plain, The Mediterranean Area, and The Alpine Area. In these cultural areas, the family is a very important part of life in Europe, and are often loyal and closely bonded.

It can therefore be surmised that the dominant Christian values and strong family orientation supposes that there is a high level of encouragement in this culture, but whether beneficiaries of such encouragement extend outside the nuclear families is another matter altogether.

North America: The dominant countries in North America are the United States of America, Canada, and Mexico. Christianity is the largest religion in the United States, Canada, and Mexico. According to a 2012 Pew Research Center survey, 77.4% of the population considered themselves Christians, so also in the 23 dependent territories in North America.

Culturally, the United States is one of the most culturally diverse countries in the world. Nearly every region of the world has influenced American culture, as it is a country of immigrants, most notably the English who colonized the country beginning in the early 1600s. US culture has also been shaped by the cultures of Native Americans, Latin Americans, Africans, and Asians.

Both Canada and the United States have shared cultural and linguistic heritage originating in Europe, and as such some points of traditional European etiquette apply to both, especially in more formal settings; however, each has formed their own etiquettes as well.

The American culture prides itself on its individualism, the way of life is very personal and depends largely on the individual or family. Regarding human relations, we must point out that most Americans, as well as Canadians, are very accommodating people, which is an aspect of encouragement. However, with the entrenched respect for individualism, is an attractive team spirit to work together for the common goal. 1 Corinthians 12:20: "But now indeed there are many members, yet one body," best describes the cultural perspective in America, where different people team up for a unified force and victory.

South America: South Americans are culturally influenced by their indigenous peoples, the historic connection with the Iberian Peninsula and Africa, and waves of immigrants from around the globe.

Because of South America's broad ethnic mix, South American cuisine has African, South American Indian, Asian, and European influences. Bahia, Brazil, is especially well known for its West African–influenced cuisine. Spanish and Portuguese are the most spoken languages in South America, with approximately 200 million speakers each. Spanish is the official language of most countries, along with other native languages in some countries. Portuguese is the official language of Brazil.

South Americans are majorly Christians and primarily Roman Catholic, and their family unit is of great importance regarding social structure. Throughout the continent, the father is considered the family head, and the mother's importance is respected as well.

When meeting and greeting, South Americans are often warm, friendly people and look for reciprocation from visitors. Common greetings include a handshake, hug, or a kiss on the right cheek. Visitors should greet the head of the household or a senior individual first. Chileans stand closer to others than most North Americans or Europeans, and it is considered rude to back away. It is also considered rude to click your fingers or beckon with an index finger.

As people that are predominantly Christians and the family as the center of their universe, and with extended family still given prominence, it is safe to say that the culture of encouragement would reign at least primarily to family members and by extension to others outside the nuclear family. The scriptures spoke of Cornelius in Acts 10:2 this way:

"He and all his family were devout and God-fearing; he gave generously to those in need and prayed to God regularly."

If therefore the same generosity is extended to those outside the nuclear family as in the case of Cornelius above, then South Americans could be said to be high on encouragement. Charity, they say, begins at home, but by Christian values, it should also be extended outside the home to all and sundry.

Asia: Asia is the largest and most populous continent, with 53 countries, including Russia, which lie in both Europe and Asia. It is the birthplace of all the world's major religions: Buddhism, Christianity, Hinduism, and Judaism, and indeed many minor ones. Judaism is the oldest of the Abrahamic faiths, and is practiced primarily in Israel --the birthplace and historical homeland of the Hebrew nation.

Christianity is a widespread religion in Asia with more than 286 million adherents, according to the Pew Research Center in 2010.

In their way of life, unlike Americans, Asians tend to be highly group-oriented people who place a strong emphasis on the family connection as the major source of identity and protection against the hardships of life.

The family model is an extended one, including immediate family and relatives, and loyalty to the family is expected. This way, independent behavior that may disrupt the harmony of the family is highly discouraged. One must never bring dishonor or disgrace to one's self or the family.

In the traditional Asian family, parents define the law, and the children are expected to abide by their requests and demands; filial piety or respect for one's parents and elders is critically important. In the most traditional of families this manifests in rules of conduct such as only speak when spoken to, or speak only if one has something important to say.

In a continent with as many as 53 countries, it is impractical to have a domineering culture, rather what exists is a diverse set of cultures depending on the individual's particular place of origin.

In this direction, therefore, it is safe not to generalize cultural values, especially as it concerns spirit of encouragement. But suffice it to say that in a culture with strong emphasis on family connection, there is wont to the tendency for family members to always be there for its members and bear one another's burden and build each other as instructed by apostle Paul in his letters to the Ephesians 4:2, Colossians 3:12, Galatians 3:13, and to the Thessalonians in 1 Thessalonians 5:11.

Africa: African culture is varied and manifold, changing from one country to another, and within a single country, many cultures can be discovered.

African culture has largely been influenced by other continents. This can be portrayed in the willingness to adapt to the ever- changing modern world rather than staying rooted to their static culture.

The people of the continent of Africa speak hundreds of languages, and if dialects spoken by various ethnic groups are also included, the number is much higher.

It must be pointed out that African culture is best described when seen from two geographical territories: North Africa and Sub-Saharan Africa.

Sub-Saharan Africa is, geographically, the area of the continent of Africa that lies south of the Sahara. According to the United Nations, it consists of all African countries that are fully or partially located south of the Sahara. It contrasts with North Africa whose territories are part of the League of the Arab world.

Because we have considered the Arab world in another continent, more emphasis would be placed here on sub-Saharan Africa.

Countries in Sub- Saharan Africa are largely Christians, while those above the Sahara, in North Africa, are predominantly Muslims, although there are also Muslim majorities in parts of the Horn of Africa.

Research shows that Sub-Saharan Africa is diverse, with many communities and villages, each with their own beliefs and traditions. The traditional culture here is communal; they believe that the needs of the many far outweigh an individual's needs and achievements. Basically, an individual's keep must be shared with other extended family members. Extended families are made up of various individuals and families who have shared responsibilities within the community.

This extended family is one of the core aspects of every black African community.

"An African will refer to an older person as auntie or uncle. Siblings of parents will be called father or mother rather than uncle and aunt. Cousins will be called brother or sister."

This system produces a kind of dependency culture, where a less endowed individual looks up to either the community and or uncle and aunty for encouragement and assistance. Conversely, the community or uncle would be very ready and willing to encourage an individual perceived to be disciplined and hard working.

When the above traits are tied to the Christian doctrine of being our brother's keeper, as encapsulated in Hebrews 13:1 "let brotherly love continue," it can be said that the culture of encouragement in a typical African culture is indeed high.

There are uncountable examples where communities, villages, counties have given scholarships to identified brilliant students to further studies either at home or abroad. In this culture, the first child has the natural responsibility to take on the training of other siblings either in school or trade. In this culture, an individual is only considered successful based on the number of people he/she has helped to raise their heads above water. This is also why the concept of Corporate Social Responsibility (CSR) which refers to business practices involving initiatives that benefit society is very important in sub- Saharan Africa. A business's CSR can encompass a wide variety of tactics, from giving away a portion of a company's proceeds to charity, to implementing "greener" business operations.

This culture of looking out for the next person as practiced is rooted in Genesis chapter 4 where God asked Cain, where is your brother Abel and Cain answered, "am I my brothers' keeper?" In black Africa, people encourage one another to live up to that cultural mandate of being a brother's keeper.

In concluding this chapter on the cultural dimension of encouragement, keep in mind that the synopsis between diverse cultures and encouragement are entirely generalized as individuals may deviate from specific cultural norms for many reasons. Again, we did not use any empirical analysis, and the degree to which cultural values are adopted by individuals is not a given.

Rather the general framework and relationship between culture and encouragement are meant to assist readers in their evangelism. There are no hard and fast rules about interacting with anyone from any part of the globe because that would lead to stereotyping which is not the aim of this chapter.

CHAPTER EIGHT

A Life of Service as an Encourager

'May our Lord Jesus Christ himself and God our Father, who loved us and by his grace gave us eternal encouragement and good hope, encourage your hearts and strengthen you in every good deed and word."
2 Thessalonians 2:16-17

It is very good to be successful in life. However, success could mean different things to different people. To some people, success is expressed in properties acquired, to others it is in positioned attained. Others see success from their level of education, in the innovations they introduced, in being an ideal parent, and a few in the number of people they inspire.

What is the yardstick for which you define success or self- actualization? It does not matter where you are on

Abraham Maslow's hierarchy of needs, either at the baseline physiological state where you are looking for necessities of life, or at the peak, where you have self-actualized, a God-fearing life requires that you must be involved in service to the Lord to guarantee success.

Service in His vineyard and specially to encourage people in the Lord Jesus Christ, is still an essential part of the job description of a good Christian. Therefore, as Christians, our definition of success must include serving others.

President George Bush senior, once said that, "Any definition of a successful life must include serving others."

We must make every effort to ensure that the goodness of the Lord gets to others through us; we must strive to be that instrument of grace, of peace, and of unity.

Rick Warren, author of best-selling inspirational books, believes that, "You will never enjoy life fully the way God intended for you to live, until you learn that it's not about you, but about a life of service to others."

This is because serving is such an important part of what life is all about, if we are to be fulfilled. Instances abound in life situations where wealth, as good as it may be, does not bring fulfillment. This fact is also true as possession of temporal power or having strong cerebral capacity.

Randy Bataanon, a non-denominational pastor, puts it this way:

"You can be as wealthy and genius as Solomon, yet feel that your life is a mistake! You can have the strength of Samson, yet live like a failure! You can have the power of Herod, yet unhappy, discontented and lost! You can have a high position like Pilate, yet confused and unsafe! You can have the handsome face of Absalom, yet unsatisfied and empty! You can have the kingdom of King Darius and yet helpless and insecure!"

To the discerning mind, the statements above may sound scary, but they are true. The only fulfilling experience any person can have is accomplishing the very purpose of God in his or her life.

Jesus laid the good example of service, and His apostles and disciples followed suit. We must place ourselves on a continuum within which we ascertain how we are faring and we will judge how we can better provide the services that will encourage one another in Christ.

Jesus offered a practical example. He even summarized his mission saying, "For even the Son of Man came not to be served but to serve, and to give His life as a ransom for many." Mark 10:45

This is what every Christian and believer is called to do. Jesus set the example already, and we must emulate our master. If you are a Christian, then you must be Christ-like.

The assignment to encourage others in Christ through our service cuts across class; it does not matter our position, especially in the ministry. These days some senior pastors relegate evangelism and reaching out to other members of the church; they get busy with administration, and when they do venture out, they target those visitations that would yield good honorariums.

To these "big men/women," Jesus said they have received their rewards already. If Jesus, with all glory with God the father, could stoop to become human and served, then such "big men" of God have totally missed it.

The Apostle Paul mentioned this problem in his letter to the Philippians:

"Let this mind be in you which was also in Christ Jesus, who, being in the form of God, did not consider it robbery to be equal with God, but made Himself of no reputation, taking the form of a bondservant, and coming in the likeness of men." Philippians 2:5-7

Jesus not only served, he also encouraged His disciples to serve:

"And He sat down, called the twelve, and said to them, "If anyone desires to be first, he shall be last of all and servant of all." Mark 9:35

The scripture says *these things happen to us as examples* (1 Corinthians 10:11). Jesus gave a perfect example; the apostles of old heeded his instruction by living a life of service as an encouragement to the brethren.

Now, Jesus did give the example and left. The Bible is replete with instances of how the men of God in both the old and New Testament encouraged others, many times, even in the face of adversity.

From the Major Prophets, to the Minor Prophets, to the disciples, they were all inspired to serve and encourage the people in their own peculiar ways, through words and actions.

Moses' humility was exemplary; David's love and fear of God was incomparable; Esther's boldness was remarkable; Hannah's confidence in God was infectious; Samuel and Ruth's commitment were awesome; Job's faith was unimaginable; Daniel's excellence was admirable; Zachariah's service even at old age, was commendable; and the list goes on.

In the New Testament, the zeal of the disciples had never been seen anywhere, just as Paul's letters to the churches are still inspiring to date.

This exemplary life of service to encourage others was not restricted to the listed twelve apostles. There were indeed other disciples, take Ananias for example; the story of the transformation of Saul to Paul cannot be complete without the mention of Ananias (Acts 9:1-19).

Saul, who was notorious for persecuting Christians, departed Jerusalem after obtaining a letter granting him authority to arrest Christians he could find in Damascus. He was to bring these believers in chains to Jerusalem for trial; but, on his way to carry out this devilish plan, he was struck down by a fierce light from heaven.

He became incapacitated and a voice spoke to him about his persecution of Christians. At the same time, the Lord appeared to Ananias in a vision and instructed him, saying, "Arise and go to the street called Straight and inquire at the house of Judas for one called Saul of Tarsus, for behold, he is praying. And in a vision, he has seen a man named Ananias coming in and putting his hand on him, so that he might receive his sight." Acts 9:11

Scared by Saul's atrocities against Christians, Ananias was afraid to go; but he could not tell God no. God insisted that Ananias was the instrument and Ananias eventually obeyed and went to minister to Saul.

On arrival at the house, Saul, being blind, had not eaten nor drank for three days:

"Ananias went his way and entered the house, and laying his hands on him he said, brother Saul, the Lord Jesus who appeared to you on the road as you came, has sent me that you may receive your sight and be filled with the Holy Spirit." Acts 9:17

Saul immediately received his sight, he got up from the floor where he has been lying for three days, he was baptized, he ate, and he joined the ministry of Jesus Christ.

Tim Challies, a Christian blogger, described the service of Ananias this way:

"At this point, Ananias fades from the story and we hear of him no more. His role in the drama of Acts is small, yet significant. We see a man who wavered when he heard God's voice, yet despite his initial hesitation he was faithful and obedient. While at first, he thought he might have to correct God, in the end he submitted himself and his very life to God's call. God then used this man to further His purposes in launching the career of the most influential of the apostles. Ananias' small act of obedience (and service), led to a great harvest for the kingdom."

Undoubtedly, Ananias' reassuring words were just what Saul needed at that moment and time, they were of great comfort to Saul.

There is even another powerful perspective here as advanced by Leslie Schwart, who observed that, "Sometimes we are presented with opportunities to encourage people we don't even know. Sometimes we will face people who have hurt us in the past. If Ananias had not been willing to take on the role of an encourager, even to a killer and evil person, the story of Saul and his conversion may have been very different. Therefore, we too, must be willing to encourage those we are not fond of, because they are often the people we can impact the most."

But even more impactful, is the example of one whose life of service as an encourager caused his colleagues to brand him "encouragement"; his name is Barnabas.

Barnabas, whose native Hebrew name was Joseph, was nicknamed, 'Son of Encouragement," by his fellow apostles, due to his charitable nature.

"And Joses who was also named Barnabas by the apostles (which is translated Son of Encouragement), a Levite of the country of Cyprus," Acts 4:36.

He excelled in encouraging others. Today, he would have been called Mr. Encouragement.

In outlining his many encouraging acts, it is imperative to point out that Barnabas was first mentioned in the scriptures as a landowner in Acts 4:36-37. He sold some land and generously donated all the proceeds from the sale to the apostles for the growth of the ministry. When we remember that a second that Ananias did the same, but he and his wife cheated in the returns made to the apostles, one can see that this was not a mean feat.

In living up to his name, shortly after, in Acts 9:27, Barnabas took Saul, who became Paul, and introduced him to the other apostles, told them Paul's conversion story and how Paul preached with power at Damascus. This made the church accept and relate with Paul because they were initially afraid of him based on his previous persecution of Christians.

Also, the church must have really trusted Barnabas as a man of unalloyed service because as represented in Acts 11:22-25, they often sent him to different places to check on the church. On one occasion, he not only went to check on what was going on at the church at Antioch, but also to look for Paul. When he found Paul, he brought him to Antioch to join in the work of the ministry.

Although Paul and Barnabas eventually had their moments of disagreement, because of John Mark (Acts 15:36-41), it was not irreconcilable, as Paul later spoke graciously of Barnabas in 1 Corinthians 9:6, an indication that they had reconciled and were working together again. Barnabas' service of encouragement was apparent as represented in Acts 11:23, 15:22-31.

Generally, the scriptures described Barnabas as a kind, forgiving, compassionate, and encouraging individual. For instance, Luke, the writer of Acts, refers to Barnabas this way:

"For he was a good man, full of the Holy Spirit and of faith..." Acts 11:24

Writing on Barnabas, Martin Collins said, "Barnabas sacrificed himself to be instrumental in God's cultivation of His church."

When there is no encouragement at home, school, and church, at work, people feel unloved, unimportant, useless and even forgotten. This is not what God wants; the Lord knows His people are in need of encouragement. He therefore lived the example to us as examined earlier, the reason scriptures instruct us to "exhort one another daily, while it is called "Today," lest any of you be hardened through the deceitfulness of sin." Hebrews 3:13

Through His words, the Lord commanded that His people encourage one another because He knows we need it. We live in a broken world where there is despair, selfishness, and where sin steals our joy. Sometimes, our strength fails us, plans falter, dreams die, our resolve weakens, and our perspective dims, but encouragement comes to keep hope alive.

As Garrett Byles points out, Biblical encouragement is not focused on complementing someone's hairdo or how good their homemade salsa tastes. Although this kind of encouragement is important, scriptural encouragement is shared with the hope that it will lift someone's heart towards the Lord.

Today, we definitely need more people like Barnabas in our homes, churches, and at work. We need men, women, and children who will encourage one another. Barnabas may have made a name for himself in the Bible days through his acts of encouragement. What about you? What are you doing to encourage the next person around you?

The good thing is that living a life of service as an encouragement to others does not need any certification or long hours of indoctrination; it starts from the heart. It is living a life of love. Charity, it is often said, begins at home, the first and most important act is to show love, it is the greatest single service. Paul said, "And now abide faith, hope, love, these three, but the greatest of these is love." 1 Corinthians 13:13.

If you indeed love your neighbor as yourself, you would not despise them, you would not put them in harm's way.

Jesus said in Mathew 7:12, "Therefore, whatever you want men to do to you, do also to them, for this is the Law and the Prophets."

Now imagine how you would feel if places are changed and you are suddenly at the receiving end of your thoughtless words or actions. Remember that where charity exists, there is no place for gossip or unkind words.

Be it at home, church, at work, school, or in the community, our agape love can reach and touch people who need our help, by treating each other kindly, speaking words of comfort and not insults. So often, this service could just be that of giving or helping out with mundane tasks because as one spiritual leader famously said, "The needs of others are ever present, and each of us can do something to help someone."

Unless we lose ourselves in service to others, there is little purpose to our own lives, and the question remains, what have you done for someone today?

In emulating Barnabas, we can encourage others by practicing stewardship of money. Barnabas sold his land and brought the money and gave it to the apostle. Barnabas saw a need and was moved to meet that need. This is in line with John MacArthur's saying that:

"All Christians are but God's stewards, everything we have is on loan from the Lord, entrusted to us for a while to use in serving Him."

We should strive to let God's grace reach others through us, by responding to their needs, thus making ourselves His instrument to encourage others.

Now, one may quickly say, "but I am not wealthy, as I am even in need myself." It should be noted that giving goes beyond money. There is always more than money to give; it could be your time, skill, sincere advice, praise, or prayers. In Acts 3, for example, the disciples, Peter and John didn't give the lame beggar alms, but they gave what they had.

"Then Peter said, "Silver and gold I do not have, but what I do have I give you: In the name of Jesus Christ of Nazareth, rise up and walk." Acts 3:6

In doing anything for others, we should always have in mind that we are doing it for the Lord and not for men.

"And whatever you do, do it heartily, as to the Lord and not to men, knowing that from the Lord you will receive the reward of the inheritance; for you serve the Lord Christ." Colossians 3:23-24

Besides giving, another lifelong service we can undertake to encourage others is to build and extend friendships. When virtually everyone was afraid of Paul after his encounter with the Lord, other disciples did not want to have anything to do with him, based on how they knew him -as a persecutor of Christians. It was Barnabas that brokered the relationship.

"But Barnabas took him and brought him to the apostles, and declared unto them how he had seen the Lord in the way, and that He had spoken to him, and how he had preached boldly at Damascus in the name of Jesus." Acts 9:27

In building friendships, Gary Chapman counsels that we should learn the special ways in which others feel most valued because not everyone's emotional needs are met in the same way.

Practically, Stacy Wiebe adds that when you introduce someone, for instance, add a few words of praise for the person's abilities and accomplishments. Say something about how they have helped you or about the nature of your relationship because it is encouraging to be praised in front of others.

Stacy adds a great one here: when someone is discouraged or hurting, offer specific, practical help. If you ask, "how can I help?" The person might be at loss to answer. It is better to ask, "would it help if I...?"Or say, "I would like to…"

The list goes on: send flowers, update your address book regularly, remind fellow Christians of the specific promises of God, pray for someone and let him or her know about it, realize the power of presence and be there, show up in church, give a respectable touch, tell people how they have encouraged you, encourage other believers with a reminder of Christ's second coming and particularly do good (Philippians 4:8), and know that as a devout Christian, your life is a sermon, so be careful what you preach at any point and time.

In living a service-oriented life, it is imperative to be discerning enough to decipher between worldly consolation and consolation through Jesus Christ.

This is because it is possible, according to Martin Collins, to receive encouragement from material things, but the effect is only temporary, like taking a depressed friend out to a restaurant or buying flowers for him or her. This no doubt gives temporary relief, but Jesus warned against this when He said, "But woe to you who are rich, for you have received your comfort." Luke 6:24

Encouragement with material things from the rich are temporary and cannot compare with encouragement through Christ. Jesus Christ is our true comforter. In his second letter to the Corinthians, the Apostle Paul described Jesus as, "The God of all comfort, who comforts us in all our tribulation, that we may be able to comfort them which are in any trouble, by the comfort wherewith we ourselves are comforted of God." 2 Corinthians 1:2-3

General overseer of the Redeemed Christian Church of God, Pastor Enoch Adeboye, elaborated on this scripture recently. According to Adeboye, "In addition to knowing God as the Father and the son, you also need to know Him as God the Holy Spirit. For example, He is the source of our power Acts 1:8, a wonderful Teacher John 14:26 and a Revealer of secrets and of future John 16:13".

Although all these characteristics are wonderful, Adeboye added, "One characteristic I find so fascinating is that He is the comforter John 14:26. If you have experienced Him as the Comforter, you will be able to comfort others in their time of distress 2 Corinthians 1:4. If you have not experienced sorrow, you cannot be of much use in comforting the sorrowful. When we encounter tragedies and sorrowful situations, the best people can do is to say comforting words like, take heart, sorry. In such situations, the ministry of the comforter is needed to heal the hurt felt deep inside. Are you presently going through a sad circumstance? Are you so sorrowful that all human attempts at comforting you have failed? The Holy Spirit will reach out and comfort you today in Jesus name."

Now the question is where can we look for this encouragement from Jesus Christ the Comforter? The answer is not farfetched, it is embedded in this scripture:

"For whatever things were written before were written for our learning, that we through the patience and comfort of the Scriptures might have hope." Romans 15:4

The promise here is that through the comfort of the scriptures, we are encouraged; the scriptures give us hope, patience, and encouragement because like shared by James Mason, life can be unthinkably cruel and lonely if you try to do it all by yourself.

We should rather see life as a tennis game, where those who don't serve well end up losing. Everyone can succeed and be great because everyone can serve; when you are serving others, life becomes more meaningful.

Let us hearken to the advice of Solomon, who said, "Let love and faithfulness never leave you; bind them around your neck, write them on the tablet of your heart. Then you will win favor and a good name in the sight of God and man."

Know that you can succeed even more by helping others to succeed, therefore, on daily basis, look for ways to help others and let your definition of success include serving others.

CHAPTER NINE

Prayer points, Bible Verses, Hymns & Choruses on Encouragement

In our very busy schedules, getting a new book is one thing and getting to read them is yet another thing entirely. It is my earnest hope that you have read the previous chapters of this book and at this time, like every other thing in life, we need to seek the face of God in prayers to help us improve individually, on our approach to encouraging one another.

The act and service of encouraging the next person cannot be achieved clinically, but rather with the help of the Holy Spirit.

If you are innately interested in carrying out this divine service, then you should take it to the Lord in prayers. Remember, the song writer says, "are you weak and heavy laden; take it to the Lord in prayer."

Below is a compilation of few Holy Spirit- led prayer points to assist in seeking the face of God to equip and empower us to encourage others.

May the Lord answer our prayers.

> *First, let us thank God for the gift of life, because only the living can praise the Lord.*
>
> *Bless the Lord for His word, even through this book.*
>
> *Thank God for how you got a copy and the time to go through the entire book.*
>
> *Thank God for the instrument God used in putting the book together for mankind.*
>
> *Sincerely seek the face of God for forgiveness about your inadequacies.*
>
> *Although you are not where you want to be, thank God that you are not where you used to be, you are now forgiven, redeemed, sanctified etc.*
>
> *Tell God to make you an instrument of encouragement.*
>
> *Ask God to help you die to self-centeredness and grow in the desire to build others up.*
>
> *Ask God to make you be of great help and comfort to your neighbor.*
>
> *Pray that the Lord's spirit of comfort and encouragement should see you through every challenge you are going through.*
>
> *Lord, according to your word in 2 Corinthians 1:4, let your whisper of comfort quiet the noise of my rails in the name of Jesus.*
>
> *According to your word in 2 Corinthians 1:4, Lord when am disheartened, send me someone to cheer, when am hungry, give me someone needing food.*

In the gracious name of Jesus, I bind and uproot every source of discouragement from my life, my parents, children and relatives.

I receive renewed encouragement and confidence to start and finish any project I lay my hands on in the mighty name of Jesus.

Teach us, good Lord, to serve you as you deserve, to give, and not to count the cost, to toil, and not to ask for rest and to labor, and not to ask for any reward.

Lord, in my service, according to word in Galatians 1:10, may I not do to seek the approval of people around me, in the name of Jesus.

Lord as you recognized Abraham's obedience in Genesis 22:16, Lord please let my services catch your attention in the gracious name of Jesus.

From this they henceforth as in 1 Kings 18:46, Lord please me special strength, special grace to encourage others.

As you did with Barnabas, Lord please make me a good example of an encourager.

Lord as I dither in encouraging others, as you did with the Shunammite woman in 2 kings 4:8-17, please overrule my doubts and give me the grace to be fervent in encouraging others.

According to your word in Psalm 148:8, as I turn my eyes to you when I experience pains and am struggling, let me please experience your comfort and hope in the mighty name of Jesus.

Lord please open my eyes that I may see the need of others, open my ears that I may hear their cries, open my heart so that they need not be without relief.

Lord Jesus, bless all who serve us, who have dedicated their lives to the ministry of others.

Make me worthy O Lord, to serve our fellow men throughout the world that live and die in poverty and hunger.

My father and my God, teach me to sacrifice my comfort to others, and my desires for the sake of doing good in the mighty name of Jesus.

Lord, on daily basis, impress upon me that it is better to give than to receive, better to forget myself than to put myself forward.

Lord Jesus, please baptize my heart into a sense of the needs and conditions of all.

Lord in your power, show me where love and hope and faith are needed, and use me to bring them to these places.

Lord Jesus, according to your word in Exodus 6:9, ;let hardship in life not discourage us from your word.

Lord, according to your word in Proverbs 14:10, please root out all bitterness that could discourage me in the mighty name of Jesus.

Father please me results that will eliminate the insults of those who mock me.

Father, let the grace to return to our first love be released upon us. Rev 2:4-5

Lord, please give me the grace and power to live a life of encouraging others in the name of Jesus.

Father, release the spirit of love and encouraging others on me in the gracious name of Jesus.

Lord, give me the grace to make encouragement, a daily discipline in Jesus name.

Lord, please show me who to encourage, bring someone to my mind that you need me to reach out to in Jesus name.

Lord, in our church, create a culture of encouragement; show us tangible ways to encourage the brethren in Jesus name.

Lord, please exceed our expectations in our efforts to encourage others in Jesus name.

BIBLE VERSES ON ENCOURAGEMENT

The scripture says in 2 Timothy 3:16-17 that, "All Scripture is given by inspiration of God, and is profitable for doctrine, for reproof, for correction, for instruction in righteousness, 17 that the man of God may be complete, thoroughly equipped for every good work."

From the above, one can confidently say that words of encouragement in the Bible are given to help Christians be thoroughly equipped for every good work. The words of God are useful and indeed relevant in every part of our life, at home at work, in school, when happy, when sad, when free, in bondage and you name it. Read Psalm 119: 11.

Therefore, as Moses instructed during his valedictory speech in Deuteronomy 11:17-19, we should make every effort to, "...lay up these words of mine in your heart and in your soul, and bind them as a sign on your hand, and they shall be as frontlets between your eyes. 19 You shall teach them to your children, speaking of them when you sit in your house, when you walk by the way, when you lie down, and when you rise up. 20 And you shall write them on the doorposts of your house and on your gates, 21 that your days and the days of your children may be multiplied in the land of which the LORD swore to your fathers to give them, like the days of the heavens above the earth."

This informs why we need to end this book with Bible verses on encouragement. It is definitely not for lack of what to write, but that as Moses enjoined Joshua, "This Book of the Law shall not depart from your mouth, but you shall meditate in it day and night, that you may observe to do according to all that is written in it. For then you will make your way prosperous, and then you will have good success."

Note that the above scripture says when you have the word and meditate on it, then, "you will make your way prosperous and have good success." We have spent considerable time discussing attributes of success, this passage says it all. Mediate on the following words on encouragement and give yourself GOOD SUCCESS.

Psalm 23:4 - Even though I walk through the darkest valley, I will fear no evil, for you are with me; your rod and your staff, they comfort me.

Psalms 28:7- The LORD [is] my strength and my shield; my heart trusted in him, and I am helped: therefore my heart greatly rejoiceth; and with my song will I praise him.

Psalms 34:4 - I sought the LORD, and he heard me, and delivered me from all my fears.

Psalm 34:8 - Taste and see that the LORD is good; blessed is the one who takes refuge in him.

Psalm 34:19 - The righteous person may have many troubles, but the LORD delivers him from them all.

Psalm 37:4 - Take delight in the LORD, and he will give you the desires of your heart.

Psalm 55:22 - Cast your cares on the LORD and he will sustain you; he will never let the righteous be shaken.

Psalm 90:1 - May the favor of the Lord our God rest on us; establish the work of our hands for us—yes, establish the work of our hands.

Psalm 103:2-6 - Praise the LORD, my soul, and forget not all his benefits- who forgives all your sins and heals all your diseases, who redeems your life from the pit and crowns you with love and compassion, who satisfies your desires with good things so that your youth is renewed like the eagle's. The LORD works righteousness and justice for all the oppressed.

Psalm 119:105 - Your word is a lamp for my feet, a light on my path.

Psalm 121:1-2 - I lift up my eyes to the mountains—where does my help come from? My help comes from the LORD, the Maker of heaven and earth.

Proverbs 3:5-6 - Trust in the LORD with all your heart and lean not on your own understanding; in all your ways submit to him, and he will make your paths straight.

Proverbs 16:3 - Commit to the LORD whatever you do, and he will establish your plans.

Proverbs 18:10 - The name of the LORD is a fortified tower; the righteous run to it and are safe.

Isaiah 40:31 - But those who hope in the LORD will renew their strength. They will soar on wings like eagles; they will run and not grow weary, they will walk and not be faint.

Jeremiah 29:11 - For I know the plans I have for you," declares the LORD, "plans to prosper you and not to harm you, plans to give you hope and a future.

Matthew 11:28 - Come to me, all you who are weary and burdened, and I will give you rest.

Romans 8:28 - And we know that in all things God works for the good of those who love him who have been called according to his purpose.

Philippians 4:6 - 7 - Do not be anxious about anything, but in every situation, by prayer and petition, with thanksgiving, present your requests to God. And the peace of God, which transcends all understanding, will guard your hearts and your minds in Christ Jesus.

Hebrews 2:18 - Because he himself suffered when he was tempted, he is able to help those who are being tempted.

1 Peter 5:7 - Cast all your anxiety on him because he cares for you.

1 John 4:4 - You, dear children, are from God and have overcome them, because the one who is in you is greater than the one who is in the world.

Deuteronomy 7:9 - Know therefore that the LORD your God is God; he is the faithful God, keeping his covenant of love to a thousand generations of those who love him and keep his commandments.

Deuteronomy 31:6 - Be strong and courageous. Do not be afraid or terrified because of them, for the LORD your God goes with you; he will never leave you nor forsake you."

Deuteronomy 31:8 - The LORD himself goes before you and will be with you; he will never leave you nor forsake you. Do not be afraid; do not be discouraged."

Joshua 1:9 - Have I not commanded you? Be strong and courageous. Do not be terrified; do not be discouraged, for the LORD your God will be with you wherever you go.

Joshua 10:25 - Joshua said to them, "Do not be afraid; do not be discouraged. Be strong and courageous. This is what the LORD will do to all the enemies you are going to fight."

Psalm 9:9 - The LORD is a refuge for the oppressed, a stronghold in times of trouble.

Psalm 16:8 - I keep my eyes always on the LORD. With him at my right hand, I will not be shaken

Psalm 27:4 - One thing I ask from the LORD, this only do I seek: that I may dwell in the house of the LORD all the days of my life, to gaze on the beauty of the LORD and to seek him in his temple.

Psalm 27:14 - Wait for the LORD; be strong and take heart and wait for the LORD.

Psalm 30:6 - 7 - When I felt secure, I said, "I will never be shaken." LORD, when you favored me, you made my royal mountain stand firm; but when you hid your face, I was dismayed.

Psalm 31:3 - Since you are my rock and my fortress, for the sake of your name lead and guide me.

Psalm 31:24 - Be strong and take heart, all you who hope in the Lord.

Psalm 32:8 - I will instruct you and teach you in the way you should go; I will counsel you with my loving eye on you.

Psalm 34:22 - The LORD will rescue his servants; no one who takes refuge in him will be condemned.

Psalm 42:5 - 6 - Why, my soul, are you downcast? Why so disturbed within me? Put your hope in God, for I will yet praise him, my Savior and my God. My soul is downcast within me; therefore I will remember you from the land of the Jordan, the heights of Hermon—from Mount Mizar.

Psalm 46:1 - 3 - God is our refuge and strength, an ever - present help in trouble. Therefore we will not fear, though the earth give way and the mountains fall into the heart of the sea, though its waters roar and foam and the mountains quake with their surging.

Psalm 55:22 - Cast your cares on the LORD and he will sustain you; he will never let the righteous be shaken.

Psalm 62:6 - Truly he is my rock and my salvation; he is my fortress, I will not be shaken.

Psalm 90:17 - May the favor of the Lord our God rest on us; establish the work of our hands for us—yes, establish the work of our hands.

Psalm 118:14 - The LORD is my strength and my defense; he has become my salvation.

Psalm 119:114 - 115 - You are my refuge and my shield; I have put my hope in your word. Away from me, you evildoers, that I may keep the commands of my God!

Psalm 119:25 - I am laid low in the dust; preserve my life according to your word.

Psalm 119:50 - My comfort in my suffering is this: Your promise preserves my life.

Psalm 119:71 - It was good for me to be afflicted so that I might learn your decrees.

Psalm 120:1 - I call on the LORD in my distress, and he answers me the LORD, the Maker of heaven and earth.

Psalm 121:7 - 8 - The LORD will keep you from all harm— he will watch over your life; the LORD will watch over your coming and going both now and forevermore.

Psalm 145:18 - 19 - The LORD is near to all who call on him, to all who call on him in truth. He fulfills the desires of those who fear him; he hears their cry and saves them.

Proverbs 2:7 - He holds success in store for the upright, he is a shield to those whose walk is blameless,

Proverbs 11:25 - A generous person will prosper; whoever refreshes others will be refreshed.

Proverbs 17:17 - A friend loves at all times, and a brother is born for a time of adversity.

Isaiah 26:3 - You will keep in perfect peace those whose minds are steadfast, because they trust in you.

Isaiah 30:19 - People of Zion, who live in Jerusalem, you will weep no more. How gracious he will be when you cry for help! As soon as he hears, he will answer you.

Isaiah 41:13 - For I am the LORD your God who takes hold of your right hand and says to you, Do not fear; I will help you.

Isaiah 41:10 - So do not fear, for I am with you; do not be dismayed, for I am your God. I will strengthen you and help you; I will uphold you with my righteous right hand.

Isaiah 43:1 - But now, this is what the LORD says— he who created you, O Jacob, he who formed you, O Israel: "Fear not, for I have redeemed you; I have summoned you by name; you are mine.

Isaiah 54:17 - No weapon forged against you will prevail, and you will refute every tongue that accuses you. This is the heritage of the servants of the LORD, and this is their vindication from me," declares the LORD.

Isaiah 58:11 - The LORD will guide you always; he will satisfy your needs in a sun - scorched land and will strengthen your frame. You will be like a well - watered garden, like a spring whose waters never fail.

Lamentations 3:25 - The LORD is good to those whose hope is in him, to the one who seeks him;

Nahum 1:7 - The LORD is good, a refuge in times of trouble. He cares for those who trust in him,

Zephaniah 3:17 - The LORD your God is with you, the Mighty Warrior who saves. He will take great delight in you; in his love he will no longer rebuke you, but will rejoice over you with singing

Matthew 6:25 - 26 - Therefore I tell you, do not worry about your life, what you will eat or drink; or about your body, what you will wear. Is not life more than food, and the body more than clothes? Look at the birds of the air; they do not sow or reap or store away in barns, and yet your heavenly Father feeds them. Are you not much more valuable than they?

Matthew 6:33 - But seek first his kingdom and his righteousness, and all these things will be given to you as well.

Matthew 7:7 - 8 - Ask and it will be given to you; seek and you will find; knock and the door will be opened to you. 8 For everyone who asks receives; the one who seeks finds; and to the one who knocks, the door will be opened.

Luke 10:19 - I have given you authority to trample on snakes and scorpions and to overcome all the power of the enemy; nothing will harm you.

Luke 11:9 - 10 - So I say to you: Ask and it will be given to you; seek and you will find; knock and the door will be opened to you. For everyone who asks receives; the one who seeks finds; and to the one who knocks, the door will be opened.

John 3:16 - For God so loved the world that he gave his one and only Son, that whoever believes in him shall not perish but have eternal life.

John 6:47 - Very truly I tell you, the one who believes has eternal life.

John 14:27 - Peace I leave with you; my peace I give you. I do not give to you as the world gives. Do not let your hearts be troubled and do not be afraid.

John 15:4 - Remain in me, as I also remain in you. No branch can bear fruit by itself; it must remain in the vine. Neither can you bear fruit unless you remain in me.

John 15:13 - Greater love has no one than this: to lay down one's life for one's friends.

John 16:33 - I have told you these things, so that in me you may have peace. In this world you will have trouble. But take heart! I have overcome the world.

Ephesians 3:20 - 21 - Now to him who is able to do immeasurably more than all we ask or imagine, according to his power that is at work within us, to him be glory in the church and in Christ Jesus throughout all generations, for ever and ever! Amen.

Philippians 4:8 - Finally, brothers and sisters, whatever is true, whatever is noble, whatever is right, whatever is pure, whatever is lovely, whatever is admirable—if anything is excellent or praiseworthy—think about such things.

1 Corinthians 10:13 - No temptation has overtaken you except what is common to mankind. And God is faithful; he will not let you be tempted beyond what you can bear. But when you are tempted, he will also provide a way out so that you can endure it.

1 Corinthians 15:57 - But thanks be to God! He gives us the victory through our Lord Jesus Christ.

1 Corinthians 16:13 - Be on your guard; stand firm in the faith; be courageous; be strong.

2 Corinthians 2:14 - Now thanks be to God who always leads us in triumph in Christ.

2 Corinthians 4:8 - 9 - We are hard pressed on every side, but not crushed; perplexed, but not in despair; persecuted, but not abandoned; struck down, but not destroyed.

2 Corinthians 4:16 - 18 - Therefore we do not lose heart. Though outwardly we are wasting away, yet inwardly we are being renewed day by day. For our light and momentary troubles are achieving for us an eternal glory that far outweighs them all. So we fix our eyes not on what is seen, but on what is unseen, since what is seen is temporary, but what is unseen is eternal.

2 Corinthians 5:7 - For we live by faith, not by sight.

2 Corinthians 5:17 - Therefore, if anyone is in Christ, the new creation has come: The old has gone, the new is here!

Romans 8:6 - The mind governed by the flesh is death, but the mind governed by the Spirit is life and peace.

Romans 8:31 - What, then, shall we say in response to these things? If God is for us, who can be against us?

Romans 8:38 - 39 - For I am convinced that neither death nor life, neither angels nor demons, neither the present nor the future, nor any powers, neither height nor depth, nor anything else in all creation, will be able to separate us from the love of God that is in Christ Jesus our Lord.

Romans 15:2 - Each of us should please our neighbors for their good, to build them up.

Romans 15:4 - For everything that was written in the past was written to teach us, so that through the endurance taught in the Scriptures and the encouragement they provide we might have hope.

Romans 15:13 - Now the God of hope fill you with all joy and peace in believing, that ye may abound in hope, through the power of the Holy Ghost.

Romans 15:5 - May the God who gives endurance and encouragement give you the same attitude of mind toward each other that Christ Jesus had.

Ephesians 3:17 - 19 - So that Christ may dwell in your hearts through faith. And I pray that you, being rooted and established in love, may have power, together with all the Lord's holy people, to grasp how wide and long and high and deep is the love of Christ, and to know this love that surpasses knowledge—that you may be filled to the measure of all the fullness of God.

Ephesians 3:20 - 21 - Now to him who is able to do immeasurably more than all we ask or imagine, according to his power that is at work within us, to him be glory in the church and in Christ Jesus throughout all generations, forever and ever! Amen.

Ephesians 6:10 - 11 - Finally, be strong in the Lord and in his mighty power. Put on the full armor of God, so that you can take your stand against the devil's schemes.

Philippians 3:7 - 9 - But whatever were gains to me I now consider loss for the sake of Christ. What is more, I consider everything a loss because of the surpassing worth of knowing Christ Jesus my Lord, for whose sake I have lost all things. I consider them garbage, that I may gain Christ and be found in him, not having a righteousness of my own that comes from the law, but that which is through faith in Christ—the righteousness that comes from God on the basis of faith.

Philippians 4:19 - And my God will meet all your needs according to the riches of his glory in Christ Jesus.

Colossians 3:15 - Let the peace of Christ rule in your hearts, since as members of one body you were called to peace. And be thankful.

2 Thessalonians 3:3 - But the Lord is faithful, and he will strengthen and protect you from the evil one.

2 Timothy 1:7 - For the Spirit God gave us does not make us timid, but gives us power, love and self - discipline.

2 Timothy 4:18 - The Lord will rescue me from every evil attack and will bring me safely to his heavenly kingdom. To him be glory forever and ever. Amen.

Hebrews 3:6 - But Christ is faithful as the Son over God's house. And we are his house, if indeed we hold firmly to our confidence and the hope in which we glory.

Hebrews 4:12 - For the word of God is alive and active. Sharper than any double - edged sword, it penetrates even to dividing soul and spirit, joints and marrow; it judges the thoughts and attitudes of the heart.

Hebrews 10:19 - 23 - Therefore, brothers and sisters, since we have confidence to enter the Most Holy Place by the blood of Jesus, by a new and living way opened for us through the curtain, that is, his body, 21 and since we have a great priest over the house of God, let us draw near to God with a sincere heart and with the full assurance that faith brings, having our hearts sprinkled to cleanse us from a guilty conscience and having our bodies washed with pure water. Let us hold unswervingly to the hope we profess, for he who promised is faithful.

Hebrews 10:25 - Not forsaking the assembling of ourselves together, as the manner of some [is]; but exhorting [one another]: and so much the more, as ye see the day approaching.

Hebrews 13:5 - Keep your lives free from the love of money and be content with what you have, because God has said, "Never will I leave you; never will I forsake you."

James 1:2 - 4 - Consider it pure joy, my brothers and sisters, whenever you face trials of many kinds, because you know that the testing of your faith produces perseverance. Let perseverance finish its work so that you may be mature and complete, not lacking anything.

James 1:12 - 15 - Blessed is the man who perseveres under trial, because when he has stood the test, he will receive the crown of life that God has promised to those who love him. When tempted, no one should say, "God is tempting me." For God cannot be tempted by evil, nor does he tempt anyone; but each one is tempted when, by his own evil desire, he is dragged away and enticed. Then, after desire has conceived, it gives birth to sin; and sin, when it is full - grown, gives birth to death.

James 4:7 - 8 - Submit yourselves, then, to God. Resist the devil, and he will flee from you. Come near to God and he will come near to you. Wash your hands, you sinners, and purify your hearts, you double - minded.

1 John 4:18 - There is no fear in love. But perfect love drives out fear, because fear has to do with punishment. The one who fears is not made perfect in love.

1 John 5:14 - 15 - This is the confidence we have in approaching God: that if we ask anything according to his will, he hears us. And if we know that he hears us—whatever we ask—we know that we have what we asked of him.

Revelation 14:12 - This calls for patient endurance on the part of the people of God who keep his commands and remain faithful to Jesus.

2 Timothy 1:7 - For God hath not given us the spirit of fear; but of power, and of love, and of a sound mind.

Proverbs 30:5 - Every word of God [is] pure: he [is] a shield unto them that put their trust in him.

Mark 11:24 - Therefore I say unto you, What things so ever ye desire, when ye pray, believe that ye receive [them], and ye shall have [them].

Philippians 4:13 - I can do all things through Christ which strengthen me.

1 Thessalonians 5:9 - 11 - For God hath not appointed us to wrath, but to obtain salvation by our Lord Jesus Christ.

Psalms 126:5 - They that sow in tears shall reap in joy.

Isaiah 43:2 - When you pass through the waters,I will be with you; and when you pass through the rivers, they will not sweep over you. When you walk through the fire, you will not be burned; the flames will not set you ablaze.

1 Thessalonians 5:11 - Therefore encourage one another and build each other up, just as in fact you are doing.

2 Corinthians 1:3 - 4 - Praise be to the God and Father of our Lord Jesus Christ, the Father of compassion and the God of all comfort, who comforts us in all our troubles, so that we can comfort those in any trouble with the comfort we ourselves receive from God.

1 Corinthians 15:58 - Therefore, my dear brothers and sisters, stand firm. Let nothing move you. Always give yourselves fully to the work of the Lord, because you know that your labor in the Lord is not in vain.

Isaiah 43:4 - Since you are precious and honored in my sight, and because I love you, I will give people in exchange for you, nations in exchange for your life valuable.

Proverbs 14:23 - All hard work brings a profit, but mere talk leads only to poverty.

1 Corinthians 16:13 - Be on your guard; stand firm in the faith; be courageous; be strong.

2 Corinthians 4:17 - For our light and momentary troubles are achieving for us an eternal glory that far outweighs them all.

John 14:27 - Peace I leave with you; my peace I give you. I do not give to you as the world gives. Do not let your hearts be troubled and do not be afraid.

Romans 8:31 - What, then, shall we say in response to these things? If God is for us, who can be against us?

Psalm 90:17 - May the favor of the Lord our God rest on us; establish the work of our hands for us yes, establish the work of our hands.

Luke 12:6 - 7 - Are not five sparrows sold for two pennies? Yet not one of them is forgotten by God. Indeed, the very hairs of your head are all numbered. Don't be afraid; you are worth more than many sparrows.

2 Corinthians 8:12 - For if the willingness is there, the gift is acceptable according to what one has, not according to what one does not have.

Encouragement Hymns

Our ultimate mission on earth is to worship our God. In carrying out this solemn responsibility, a very good way of doing it is to sing unto God, songs of adoration. Psalm 29:2.

Below are few encouragement focused hymns that we can sing from our soul to worship His majesty in the beauty of His holiness.

THERE'S NOT A FRIEND LIKE THE LOWLY JESUS

There's not a Friend like the lowly Jesus:
No, not one! no, not one!
None else could heal all our souls' diseases:
No, not one! no, not one!

Jesus knows all about our struggles;
He will guide 'til the day is done:
There's not a Friend like the lowly Jesus:
No, not one! no, not one!

No friend like Him is so high and holy,
No, not one! no, not one!
And yet no friend is so meek and lowly,
No, not one! no, not one!

There's not an hour that He is not near us,
No, not one! no, not one!
No night so dark, but His love can cheer us,
No, not one! no, not one!

Did ever saint find this Friend forsake him?
No, not one! no, not one!
Or sinner find that He would not take him?
No, not one! no, not one!

Was e'er a gift like the Savior given?
No, not one! no, not one!
Will He refuse us a home in heaven?
No, not one! no, not one!

WHAT A FRIEND WE HAVE IN JESUS

1. What a friend we have in Jesus,
All our sins and griefs to bear!
What a privilege to carry
Everything to God in prayer!
Oh, what peace we often forfeit,
Oh, what needless pain we bear,
All because we do not carry
Everything to God in prayer!

2. Have we trials and temptations?
Is there trouble anywhere?
We should never be discouraged—
Take it to the Lord in prayer.
Can we find a friend so faithful,
Who will all our sorrows share?
Jesus knows our every weakness;
Take it to the Lord in prayer.

3. Are we weak and heavy - laden,
Cumbered with a load of care?
Precious Savior, still our refuge—
Take it to the Lord in prayer.
Do thy friends despise, forsake thee?
Take it to the Lord in prayer!
In His arms He'll take and shield thee,
Thou wilt find a solace there.

4. Blessed Savior, Thou hast promised
Thou wilt all our burdens bear;
May we ever, Lord, be bringing
All to Thee in earnest prayer.
Soon in glory bright, unclouded,
There will be no need for prayer—
Rapture, praise, and endless worship
Will be our sweet portion there.

ABIDE WITH ME

1. Abide with me; fast falls the eventide;
The darkness deepens; Lord, with me abide;
When other helpers fail and comforts flee,
Help of the helpless, oh, abide with me.

2. Swift to its close ebbs out life's little day;
Earth's joys grow dim, its glories pass away;
Change and decay in all around I see—
O Thou who changest not, abide with me.

3. I need Thy presence every passing hour;
What but Thy grace can foil the tempter's pow'r?
Who, like Thyself, my guide and stay can be?
Through cloud and sunshine, Lord, abide with me.

4. I fear no foe, with Thee at hand to bless;
Ills have no weight, and tears no bitterness;
Where is death's sting? Where, grave, thy victory?
I triumph still, if Thou abide with me.
5. Hold Thou Thy cross before my closing eyes;
Shine through the gloom and point me to the skies;
Heav'n's morning breaks, and earth's vain shadows flee;
In life, in death, O Lord, abide with me.

LORD, SPEAK TO ME, THAT I MAY SPEAK

1. Lord, speak to me, that I may speak
in living echoes of thy tone;
as thou has sought, so let me seek
thine erring children lost and lone.

2. O strengthen me, that while I stand
firm on the rock, and strong in thee,
I may stretch out a loving land
to wrestlers with the troubled sea.

3. O teach me, Lord, that I may teach
the precious things thou dost impart;
and wing my words, that they may reach
the hidden depths of many a heart.

4. O fill me with thy fullness, Lord,
until my very heart o'erflow
in kindling thought and glowing word,
thy love to tell, thy praise to show.

5. O use me, Lord, use even me,
just as thou wilt, and when, and where,
until thy blessed face I see,
thy rest, thy joy, thy glory share.

COURAGE BROTHER, DO NOT STUMBLE

Courage Brother, do not stumble
Though thy path be dark as night;
There's a star to guide the humble
Trust in God, and do the right.

Let the road be rough and dreary,
And its end far out of sight,
Foot it bravely, strong or weary,
Trust in God, and do the right.

Perish policy and cunning,
Perish all that fears the light;
Whether winning, whether losing,
Trust in God, and do the right.

Trust no party, sect or faction,
Trust no leaders in the fight:
But in every word and action,
Trust in God, and do the right.

Trust no lovely forms of passion,
Foes may look like angels bright,
Trust no custom, school or fashion,
Trust in God, and do the right.

Simple rule and safest guiding,
Inward peace and inward might;
Star upon our path abiding,
Trust in God, and do the right.

Some will hate thee, some will love thee,
Some will flatter, some will slight;
Cease from man, and look above thee,
Trust in God, and do the right.

WHAT A FRIEND WE HAVE IN JESUS

What a friend we have in Jesus,
All our sins and griefs to bear!
What a privilege to carry
Everything to God in prayer!
Oh, what peace we often forfeit;
Oh, what needless pain we bear
All because we do not carry
Everything to God in prayer!
Have we trials and temptations?
Is there trouble any where?
We should never be discouraged
Take it to the Lord in prayer.
Can we find a friend so faithful
Who will all our sorrows share?
Jesus knows our every weakness
Take it to the Lord in prayer.
Are we weak and heavy laden,
Cumbered with a load of care?
Precious Savior, still our refuge
Take it to the Lord in prayer.
Do your friends despise, forsake you?
Take it to the Lord in prayer.
In his arms he'll take and shield you;
You will find a solace there.

THROUGH THE LOVE OF GOD, OUR SAVIOR,

Through the love of God, our Savior,
all will be well;
free and changeless is his favor,
all will be well;
precious is the blood that healed us,
perfect is the grace that sealed us,
strong the hand stretched out to shield us,
all will be well.

Though we pass through tribulation,
all will be well;
ours is such a full salvation,
all will be well.
happy when in god confiding,
fruitful if in Christ abiding,
holy through the Spirit's guiding,
all will be well.

We expect a bright tomorrow;
all will be well;
faith can sing through days of sorrow,
all will be well;
on our Father's love relying,
Jesus every need supplying
in our living, in our dying,
all will be well.

I NEED THEE EVERY HOUR

I need Thee every hour, most gracious Lord;
No tender voice like Thine can peace afford.
Refrain
I need Thee, O I need Thee;
Every hour I need Thee;
O bless me now, my Savior,
I come to Thee.

I need Thee every hour, stay Thou nearby;
Temptations lose their power when Thou art nigh.

Refrain

I need Thee every hour, in joy or pain;
Come quickly and abide, or life is in vain.

Refrain

I need Thee every hour; teach me Thy will;
And Thy rich promises in me fulfill.

Refrain

I need Thee every hour, most Holy One;
O make me Thine indeed, Thou blessèd Son.

I need Thee every hour, most gracious Lord;
No tender voice like Thine can peace afford.

Refrain

I need Thee, O I need Thee;
Every hour I need Thee;
O bless me now, my Savior,
I come to Thee.

I need Thee every hour, stay Thou nearby;
Temptations lose their power when Thou art nigh.

Refrain

I need Thee every hour, in joy or pain;
Come quickly and abide, or life is in vain.

Refrain

I need Thee every hour; teach me Thy will;
And Thy rich promises in me fulfill.

Refrain

I need Thee every hour, most Holy One;
O make me Thine indeed, Thou blessed Son.

I AM THINE O LORD

I am Thine, O Lord, I have heard Thy voice,
And it told Thy love to me;
But I long to rise in the arms of faith
And be closer drawn to Thee.
Refrain
Draw me nearer, nearer blessed Lord,
To the cross where Thou hast died.
Draw me nearer, nearer, nearer blessed Lord,
To Thy precious, bleeding side.
Consecrate me now to Thy service, Lord,
By the power of grace divine;
Let my soul look up with a steadfast hope,
And my will be lost in Thine.
O the pure delight of a single hour
That before Thy throne I spend,
When I kneel in prayer, and with Thee, my God
I commune as friend with friend!
There are depths of love that I cannot know
Till I cross the narrow sea;
There are heights of joy that I may not reach
Till I rest in peace with Thee.

PRAYER POINTS ON ENCOURAGEMENT

PERSONAL ENCOURAGEMENT

1 Peter 5:10 - 11 - But may the God of all grace, who called us to His eternal glory by Christ Jesus, after you have suffered a while, perfect, establish, strengthen, and settle you. NKJV.

Micah 7:8 - 10 - Rejoice not against me, O mine enemy: when I fall , I shall arise; when I sit in darkness, the LORD shall be a light unto me. 9 I will bear the indignation of the LORD, because I have sinned against him, until he plead my cause, and execute judgment for me: he will bring me forth to the light, and I shall behold his righteousness.10 Then she that is mine enemy shall see it, and shame shall cover her which said unto me, Where is the LORD thy God? mine eyes shall behold her: now shall she be trodden down. KJV.

1. Almighty God, arise and strengthen me from within with all might, in the name of Jesus.

2. Holy Spirit, give me the fortitude to brace up and continue my ministry despite all odds, in the name of Jesus.

3. Lord Jesus, defend me against every enemy that is set to rejoice against me in, the name of Jesus.

4. Lord Jesus, give me victory over every force orchestrated to discourage me, in the name of Jesus.

5. Father, encourage me, establish me, and settle me early, in the name of Jesus.

6. Father, encourage me with concerted results and success in ministry, in the name of Jesus.

7. Lord Jesus, dry up my tears and put your joy into my endeavors (Nehemiah 8:10), in the name of Jesus.

8. Almighty God, replace my regrets with breakthroughs and make me dance the victory dance you promised me, in the name of Jesus.

9. Almighty God, arise and do a new thing, then put a new song in my mouth, in the name of Jesus.

10. Almighty God, let me hear your voice of hope, direction and encouragement on a daily basis as I move on in life, in the name of Jesus(Acts 22:14 - 15).

FAMILY ENCOURAGEMENT

Genesis 18:19 - For I have known him, in order that he may command his children and his household after him, that they keep the way of the LORD, to do righteousness and justice, that the LORD may bring to Abraham what He has spoken to him. NKJV.

Psalm 119:52 - 54 - I remembered Your judgments of old, O LORD, And have comforted myself. 53 Indignation has taken hold of me Because of the wicked, who forsake Your law. 54 Your statutes have been my songs in the house of my pilgrimage. NKJV.

Isaiah 48:10 - 11 - Behold, I have refined you, but not as silver; I have tested you in the furnace of affliction. 11 For My own sake, for My own sake, I will do it; For how should My name be profaned? And I will not give My glory to another. NKJV.

1. Almighty God, give my family a testimonial name, in the name of Jesus.

2. Father, give my family an encouragement of fruitfulness, in the name of Jesus.

3. Father, by the help of the Holy Spirit, give everyone in my family listening ears to your word and statutes, in the name of Jesus.

4. Father, by the help of the Holy Spirit, let everybody in my family possess a pure heart and clean hands, in the name of Jesus.

5. Lord Jesus, teach me to comfort and encourage myself in the Lord when household enemies and family storms come raging, in the name of Jesus.

6. Father, success is an incentive, please let everyone in my family succeed in all their endeavors, in the name of Jesus.

7. Father, decorate me and everyone in my family with sound health and sound mind, in the name of Jesus.

8. Almighty Jehovah, let there be no appearing of affliction in my life any more, in the name of Jesus.

9. Father, for your own sake, give me and all my loved ones a Divine expressway to the top, in the mighty name of Jesus.

10. Holy prove to the whole world that Christ in my family is a Hope of Glory by miracles, Signs and Wonders, in the name of Jesus.

ENCOURAGEMENT FOR MINISTERS AND MINISTRY LEADERS

Acts 22:12 - 15 - "Then a certain Ananias, a devout man according to the law, having a good testimony with all the Jews who dwelt there, 13 came to me; and he stood and said to me, 'Brother Saul, receive your sight.' And at that same hour I looked up at him. 14 Then he said, 'The God of our fathers has chosen you that you should know His will, and see the Just One, and hear the voice of His mouth. 15 For you will be His witness to all men of what you have seen and heard NKJV.

Isaiah 30:21 - Your ears shall hear a word behind you, saying, "This is the way, walk in it, "Whenever you turn to the right hand Or whenever you turn to the left NKJV.

Exodus 15:2 - 3 - The LORD is my strength and song, And He has become my salvation; He is my God, and I will praise Him; My father's God, and I will exalt Him. 3 The LORD is a man of war; The LORD is His name NKJV.

Exodus 15:2 - 3 - The LORD is my strength and song, And He has become my salvation; He is my God, and I will praise Him; My father's God, and I will exalt Him. 3 The LORD is a man of war; The LORD is His name NKJV.

1 Kings 19:5 - 8 - Then as he lay and slept under a broom tree, suddenly an angel touched him, and said to him, "Arise and eat." 6 Then he looked, and there by his head was a cake baked on coals, and a jar of water. So he ate and drank, and lay down again. 7 And the angel of the LORD came back the second time, and touched him, and said, "Arise and eat, because the journey is too great for you." 8 So he arose, and ate and drank; and he went in the strength of that food forty days and forty nights as far as Horeb, the mountain of God NKJV.

1. My Father and my Caller, please let me hear your voice of encouragement and comfort in the midst of my weariness, in the name of Jesus.

2. Father, give me your counsel and direction so that I will not walk into discouragement and weariness, in the name of Jesus.

3. Holy Spirit, keep me in the Will of My God at all times as I do the Work of the Ministry, in the name of Jesus.

4. My Lord and My Strength, back me up in all the battles that I face in life and ministry, in the name of Jesus.

5. Almighty God, give me reasons to praise your name every morning; and offer thanksgiving to you every evening of my life, in the name of Jesus.

6. Father, convert every weariness that the Devil brings my way into strength by your Grace, in the name of Jesus.

7. My Lord and My Helper, see me through every journey that seems too great for me and my physical strength, in the name of Jesus.

8. Almighty God give me the wisdom to rule and reign in

every place and every height you take me, in the name of Jesus (1 Chronicles 1:10).

9. Almighty Father, give me the tongue of the Learned so that I may declare your Counsel a right to every man, in the name of Jesus.

10. Father, encourage me and strengthen me to finish well and strong, in the name of Jesus.

ENCOURAGEMENT FOR MISSIONARIES

Romans 8:35 - 39 - Who shall separate us from the love of Christ? Shall tribulation, or distress, or persecution, or famine, or nakedness, or peril, or sword? 36 As it is written: "For Your sake we are killed all day long; We are accounted as sheep for the slaughter." 37 Yet in all these things we are more than conquerors through Him who loved us. 38 For I am persuaded that neither death nor life, nor angels nor principalities nor powers, nor things present nor things to come, 39 nor height nor depth, nor any other created thing, shall be able to separate us from the love of God which is in Christ Jesus our Lord NKJV.

2 Corinthians 11:26 - 29 - In journeys often, in perils of waters, in perils of robbers, in perils of my own countrymen, in perils of the Gentiles, in perils in the city, in perils in the wilderness, in perils in the sea, in perils among false brethren; 27 in weariness and toil, in sleeplessness often, in hunger and thirst, in fastings often, in cold and nakedness — 28 besides the other things, what comes upon me daily: my deep concern for all the churches NKJV.

1. Holy Spirit, let no discouragement or affliction break me away from the Most High God, in the name of Jesus.

2. Father, encourage me with victories and keep me to me more than a conqueror, in the name of Jesus.

3. Almighty God, equip me with Heavenly gadgets so that

no evil arrow may penetrate my life and the lives of my loved ones, in the name of Jesus.

4. Father, reward me appropriately in this mission work and let me not lack and good thing, in the name of Jesus.

5. Father, let your protective hand be with me in all terrains and territories, in the name of Jesus.

6. Lord Jesus, let my weariness and toiling take me to my prepared blessing in ministry, in the name of Jesus.

7. Father, through thick and thin, ups and downs, prove that you are with me, in the name of Jesus.

8. Lord Jesus as I pray and fast, comfort me with deliverance and victory, in the name of Jesus.

9. Holy Spirit, help me to scale all impediments on my way to mission enlargement, in the name of Jesus.

10. Father, as I seek your kingdom and its righteousness, let every other good thing be added unto me, in the name of Jesus.

ENCOURAGEMENT FOR LEADERS IN GOVERNMENT AND ORGANIZATIONS

Isaiah 50:4 - "The Lord GOD has given Me The tongue of the learned, That I should know how to speak A word in season to him who is weary He awakens Me morning by morning, He awakens My ear To hear as the learned NKJV.

Proverbs 29:2 - When the righteous are in authority, the people rejoice; But when a wicked man rules, the people groan NKJV.

Luke 21:15 - 16 - For I will give you a mouth and wisdom which all your adversaries will not be able to contradict or resist NKJV.

1. Almighty give me the tongue of the learned to manage and lead your people to achievement and success, in the name of Jesus.

2. Great and Mighty God, please take care of every antagonist in my domain and territory, in the name of Jesus.

3. Almighty God, give the wisdom and utterance to defeat every type of Pharisee and Sadducee that my rise against me as I lead your people, in the name of Jesus.

4. Holy Spirit, give me the right Word of encouragement for your people at all times and in every situation, in the name of Jesus.

5. Lord Jesus, let the Spirit of joy dominate my ministry, regime, and jurisdiction to the Glory of your name, in the name of Jesus.

6. Father, let your peace and your love rule and reign in my administration to the Glory of your holy name, in the name of Jesus.

7. Almighty God, by the reason of signs and Wonders, keep all forms of pains and groaning far from my regime, ministry, and business, in the name of Jesus.

8. Father, season my voice and word with your power so that no adversary will resist me, in the name of Jesus.

9. Father, give me the strength, zeal, and wisdom to eliminate every discouraging contradiction in home, work, and ministry, in the name of Jesus.

10. Almighty God, let it be well with me and make me your testimony of righteousness and accountability, in the name of Jesus.

FINANCIAL ENCOURAGEMENT IN TIMES LIKE THIS

Ecclesiastes 7:12 - For wisdom is a defense as money is a defense,

But the excellence of knowledge is that wisdom gives life to those who have it NKJV.

Ecclesiastes 10:19 - A feast is made for laughter, and wine maketh glad the life; and money answereth all things. ASV.

Psalm 34:5 - 6 - They looked to Him and were radiant, And their faces were not ashamed. 6 This poor man cried out, and the LORD heard him, and saved him out of all his troubles. NKJV.

1. Father, give me prominence by financial stability, in the name of Jesus.

2. Almighty God, let my voice be respected in the places of money, in the name of Jesus.

3. Father, from now on let finances not be a limitation in family and ministry operations for me, in the name of Jesus.

4. Father, as a means of Divine encouragement, raise financial helpers for me, my family, and Ministry, in the name of Jesus.

5. Lord Jesus, cancel every moment of financial sorrows and embarrassment finally in my life, in the name of Jesus.

6. Almighty God, the Great Provider, establish my financial base to the extent that my head will never again be bowed down in sorrow, in the name of Jesus.

7. Father, let everyone around me and my loved ones begin to enjoy financial and material peace and satisfaction, in the name of Jesus.

8. Father, today I ask for blessings of the Lord that has no sorrow with it to begin to come at my beck and call, in the name of Jesus.

9. Father in my Ministry, family, and businesses, let me begin to send money on errand, in the Mighty name of Jesus.

10. Today, O Lord, I ask for the anointing to speak the grace and favor to get wealth into the lives of people. Release it to me, in the name of Jesus.

Be Encouraged until He comes in the name of Jesus.

ABOUT JAMES O. FADEL

Born on April 5, 1958, into a devout Catholic family, Pastor Fadel, as he is fondly called, tells of how he carried his father's Bible on his head as they went to church every Sunday. After he graduated with honors in junior college education in Nigeria, he relocated to the United States in 1982 on a Nigerian - Western State study scholarship. Pastor Fadel received a bachelor's degree in Mechanical Engineering and Applied Mathematics from the Western Michigan University in 1986 and also achieved a successful professional career with the Ford Motor Company as a Mechanical Engineer.

Rising to the position of Senior Design Engineer with key achievements in lead positions, he later obtained a Master of Science degree in Operations Research from Wayne State University in 1990, followed by a MBA degree from the Lawrence Technological University, Michigan in 1993. He continued with subsequent entrepreneurial achievements in metropolitan Detroit. In 2012, he completed his Doctorate degree and earned a Doctor of Ministry (D.Min) from Bakke Graduate University.

Having committed his life to the Lord in 1973, Pastor Fadel joined The Redeemed Christian Church of God (RCCG) in Nigeria in 1975 and continued to serve the Lord in the US with a passion that culminated in a call to ministry. He also attended the Bible College of Birmingham in order to prepare himself for what he knew was God's purpose for his life.

Mentored by the General Overseer of RCCG, Pastor E.A. Adeboye, Pastor Fadel pioneered a home fellowship in his basement in 1991. By 1992, this developed into the first parish of RCCG in North America – Winner's Chapel, Detroit. In 2001, Pastor Fadel was appointed the Chairman, Board of Coordinators of RCCGNA.

Under his leadership, RCCGNA has grown to over 800 parishes in 117 zones. Each year, thousands attend the annual RCCGNA convention at the over 700-acre campground in Floyd, Texas. Pastor Fadel also works tirelessly to develop other national programs to enable RCCGNA ministers and workers to develop and mature in their Christian walk and service.

By the grace of God, he is happily married to Pastor Manita, a medical doctor specializing in the area of pediatric medicine, and they are blessed with three children.

ENCOURAGEMENT:

Something Everyone Needs!

In real life, everyone hurts, everyone gets challenged, and everyone gets beaten up by one situation or another. It's said that the challenges, problems, predicaments, troubles, trials, and tribulations of life are no respecter of persons: "The rich also cry!" We all, without exception, go through situations in life; though what we go through may differ in timing, degree, nature, or nomenclature. For this reason, the subject under discussion is relevant and appropriate, especially today. It's something everyone needs!

The Author, Dr. Fadel, in this compelling book, has rightly concluded that encouragement is a ministry for all believers. Opening this book, it was difficult for me to put it down until I finished reading it. I saw encouragement in a different perspective, as a "faith booster," a "spiritual alchemy", "cure-all spiritual pharmaceutical", or "spiritual therapy," for all situations of life! I believe this book will be of significant help to the body of Christ at this time, and I pray it ministers encouragement to an individual or family going through a situation that may be difficult to bear and hard to comprehend at this moment. In Jesus name, Amen.

Pastor OJ Kuye
RCCG House on the Rock
Grand Prairie, Dallas TX

OTHER BOOKS BY PASTOR FADEL

YOUR 4 FATHERS

Pastor (Dr.) Fadel has written a book to change the society. "Your 4 Fathers and Their Kingdoms" is a strategic message to a nation in need. It is a book written to bring order at a prophetic level into the fabrics of the nations. It seeks to redress the challenge that Pastor John Hagee succinctly describes in the foreword, "Our society is crumbling from within because the role of the father as priest, prophet, provider and protector has been removed."

The book prescribed a solution to this problem by defining and highlighting the calling and impact of the 4 types of fathers that everyone should have: A Biological Father, Tutorial Father, Spiritual Father and a Heavenly Father.

"Your 4 Fathers & Their Kingdoms" is useful as a text in matters dealing with families and leadership at every layer of the society. It is a must-read for every discerning heart.

Available on Amazon.com and other top book stores.